797,885 Books

are available to read at

www.ForgottenBooks.com

Forgotten Books' App
Available for mobile, tablet & eReader

ISBN 978-1-331-37082-6
PIBN 10180628

This book is a reproduction of an important historical work. Forgotten Books uses state-of-the-art technology to digitally reconstruct the work, preserving the original format whilst repairing imperfections present in the aged copy. In rare cases, an imperfection in the original, such as a blemish or missing page, may be replicated in our edition. We do, however, repair the vast majority of imperfections successfully; any imperfections that remain are intentionally left to preserve the state of such historical works.

Forgotten Books is a registered trademark of FB &c Ltd.
Copyright © 2015 FB &c Ltd.
FB &c Ltd, Dalton House, 60 Windsor Avenue, London, SW19 2RR.
Company number 08720141. Registered in England and Wales.

For support please visit www.forgottenbooks.com

1 MONTH OF FREE READING

at

www.ForgottenBooks.com

By purchasing this book you are eligible for one month membership to ForgottenBooks.com, giving you unlimited access to our entire collection of over 700,000 titles via our web site and mobile apps.

To claim your free month visit:

www.forgottenbooks.com/free180628

* Offer is valid for 45 days from date of purchase. Terms and conditions apply.

Similar Books Are Available from
www.forgottenbooks.com

Beautiful Joe
An Autobiography, by Marshall Saunders

Theodore Roosevelt, an Autobiography
by Theodore Roosevelt

Napoleon
A Biographical Study, by Max Lenz

Up from Slavery
An Autobiography, by Booker T. Washington

Gotama Buddha
A Biography, Based on the Canonical Books of the Theravādin, by Kenneth J. Saunders

Plato's Biography of Socrates
by A. E. Taylor

Cicero
A Biography, by Torsten Petersson

Madam Guyon
An Autobiography, by Jeanne Marie Bouvier De La Motte Guyon

The Writings of Thomas Jefferson
by Thomas Jefferson

Thomas Skinner, M.D.
A Biographical Sketch, by John H. Clarke

Saint Thomas Aquinas of the Order of Preachers (1225-1274)
A Biographical Study of the Angelic Doctor, by Placid Conway

Recollections of the Rev. John Johnson and His Home
An Autobiography, by Susannah Johnson

Biographical Sketches in Cornwall, Vol. 1 of 3
by R. Polwhele

Autobiography of John Francis Hylan, Mayor of New York
by John Francis Hylan

The Autobiography of Benjamin Franklin
The Unmutilated and Correct Version, by Benjamin Franklin

James Mill
A Biography, by Alexander Bain

George Washington
An Historical Biography, by Horace E. Scudder

Florence Nightingale
A Biography, by Irene Cooper Willis

Marse Henry
An Autobiography, by Henry Watterson

Autobiography and Poems
by Charlotte E. Linden

Thomson.

THE RT. HON. H. H. ASQUITH, P.C., D.C.L., LL.D.

HERBERT HENRY ASQUITH

BY
HAROLD SPENDER

LONDON
GEORGE NEWNES, LIMITED

PREFACE

In time of war there is every need to tell the people all that can be told about their leaders. For loyal following is the condition of effective leadership, itself essential to success in war. But the blind cannot follow. The people must have a vision of their leaders if they are to be true to them. Otherwise loyalty withers from sheer lack of food.

It is sometimes our best who suffer most from such a famine of the human heart. For it is often the finest temperaments that shrink to-day from that fierce light which now daily and hourly beats upon the thrones of power.

And yet it is vital that these leaders of ours should be known to us. For they are the banner-bearers in this great contention of mind and matter which to-day divides the world. On them rest the hopes of the people. They hold the springs of defeat or victory.

"There shall be a time of trouble," said a great prophet of the ancient world,* "such as never was since there was a nation even to that same time" In that trouble—he went on to say—"they that be wise shall shine as the brightness of the firmament."

It is such a beacon of wisdom, surely, that the world needs now to lighten the thick gloom, as of a darkness palpable and visible, which enshrouds the future of mankind.

In other ages the world would have sought that light from prophets or saints. That is not our habit to-day. Now, as in the days of Ahab, we only listen to the prophets when they prophesy smooth things. Otherwise, we smite them on the cheek.†

It is to-day our habit in secular matters to turn to secular guides. The saints and prophets have had their day in the affairs of this world. Our modern way is to look for worldly guidance to trained men of affairs of proved integrity and judgment. In matters of State, we consult the statesmen.

Among the men who have a claim to that high and rare title, Mr. Asquith stands pre-eminent in Western Europe. Both by length of training

---

* Daniel xii. 1-4. † 1 Kings xxii. 24.

and proved efficiency, he has established a golden lien on our confidence. He has recently guided us through a great constitutional crisis. To-day there is laid upon him an even greater task. But the qualities of coolness, fidelity, and endurance which he has before so often displayed, are just such as are required for national leading in time of war. It has been in the past thus —by such qualities—that the great Pilots, men like Pitt and Lincoln, have steered nations through such hurricanes.

This is no official record or family biography. The time for such a task is happily not yet. This is a sketch of a career fortunately still unfinished : an attempt to appreciate a personality still glowing on the anvil of this iron world. But the sketch, such as it is, contains many new details of Mr. Asquith's life : and in every case I have taken every available means to sift and verify.

H. S.

LONDON,
September 14, 1915.

CONTENTS

CHAPTER		PAGE
I.	BOYHOOD	1
II.	UNIVERSITY CAREER (1870-74)	17
III.	FROM COLLEGE TO PARLIAMENT	34
IV.	PARLIAMENT	48
V.	HOME SECRETARY	64
VI.	OPPOSITION—THE SOUTH AFRICAN WAR	84
VII.	OPPOSITION—FREE TRADE	99
VIII.	CHANCELLOR AND PRIME MINISTER	111
IX.	CIVIL STRIFE AND FOREIGN WAR	125
X.	CHARACTERISTICS	142

HERBERT HENRY ASQUITH

CHAPTER I

BOYHOOD

"And there remain Iron, Wool, and Cotton, but the greatest of these is Wool."—*Anon.*

HERBERT HENRY ASQUITH was born on the twelfth day of September, 1852, in "Croft House" at Morley, in the West Riding of Yorkshire. Thus the future Prime Minister of the British Empire first saw the light of day in what was then a small township at the very heart of industrial England. For Morley lies in the midst of that throbbing district between Bradford and Leeds, where the leading of the people is now, as of old, a pillar of cloud by day and a pillar of fire by night.

Mr. Asquith has always been proud of his county and village. He has never been ashamed to own himself a Yorkshireman. Speaking to the neighbours of his childhood at the height of his career, when he opened the townhall at

Morley, now a full-grown town, in 1895, Mr. Asquith said :—

> "They would not be worse but better Englishmen because among Englishmen they were proud to belong to Yorkshire, and because in Yorkshire they were proud to belong to the West Riding, and because among men of the West Riding they were proud to belong to Morley."

In the same speech Mr. Asquith told an interesting story of his ancestry. In 1664 one Joseph Asquith, a stout Puritan, made a pathetic and forlorn attempt to set up on a small scale a revival of that great Puritan Commonwealth which had perished so soon after the death of its founder some years before. It was an attempt known in history as the Farnley Wood Plot. Joseph Asquith was captured by the soldiers of Charles II.; and sentenced to be hanged, drawn and quartered. Mr. Asquith in 1895 told his Morley friends, doubtless with a humorous twinkle in his eye, how, as Home Secretary, he had painfully hunted in the records of the Home Office but failed to find any record that the sentence had been interfered with. Mr. Asquith manfully gloried in this ancestry, as showing that he was descended from men who knew how to die for their faith. It seems a sufficiently good pedigree for a moulder of our modern liberties.

Mr. Gladstone, it has been well said, was the joint result of Cotton and Oxford. In the same sense and spirit, Mr. Asquith may claim as his foster-parents Oxford and Wool—but perhaps chiefly Wool.

For Mr. Asquith's grandfather and father were giving their whole energies to the woollen business just at that halcyon time, when Free Trade was releasing the cribbed and cabined energies of the Midlands and the North, and when the expansion of the new railway system was providing those energies with a wider and swifter reach. It was, in Yorkshire, a time of conquering energy rising from a soil of sturdy independence and simple living. These men of the North, conscious of their new powers, were not inclined to accept dictation from either State or Church. The manufacturers of the West Riding formed a stout and solid barrier of resistance to the rally of reactionary hopes which followed on the great achievements of the generation of the great Reform Act.

Mr. Asquith's father was Mr. Joseph Dixon Asquith, the founder of the Gillroyd Mill Company at Morley, himself the son of Mr. Joseph Asquith, also a woollen manufacturer. Both were stalwart

Nonconformists of the Congregationalist persuasion, and held the political views which generations of struggle for freedom have engrafted on that faith. But the purely political interests of the family were greatly deepened and strengthened by the fact that Mr. Joseph Dixon Asquith married a daughter of that remarkable man, Mr. William Willans, of Huddersfield. Mr. Willans was a very strong and pugnacious Radical, a fighting Congregationalist who allowed his goods to be distrained upon in the great historic struggle of the mid-century against Church Rates. Mr. Willans was a friend of men like Sir Francis Crossley and Sir Titus Salt, the leaders of Yorkshire Radicalism; and he was sufficiently prominent in the Yorkshire political world to stand for Parliament. Mr. Willans had eight children, and Mrs. Joseph Dixon Asquith was perhaps the cleverest of the girls. She became the mother of three children, the first two of them boys and the third a girl, all of them still living.* The second of these children is now "Mr. Asquith."

It was when the young Asquith was eight years

---

* The elder brother, Mr. W. W. Asquith, was for thirty-five years a schoolmaster at Clifton College, and now lives in Hampstead; the girl became Mrs. Wooding, and lives in North London. There were also two little girls who died in infancy.

of age (1860) that there fell upon this little family the worst of human calamities, the death of the father and breadwinner in the prime of life (thirty-five), before the children were old enough to support themselves. This early death of a much-loved husband naturally came as a great shock to Mr. Asquith's mother, and she seems never to have entirely recovered from the blow. The home, recently moved from Morley to Mirfield, was now broken up. Mrs. Asquith went to live near her father at Huddersfield. The paternal grandfather had died before his son, and the Asquith boys were now largely left to the dutiful guardianship of the Willans grandfather and uncles.

For the first three years—from Mr. Asquith's ninth to his twelfth year—this task was performed by the grandfather, Mr. Willans. He sent the boys to the Fulneck school, in Yorkshire. This school is part of an English settlement of that remarkable religious community known from their country of origin by the name of Moravians, the scattered descendants of the earliest and purest European Protestants, the followers of Huss. The Pudsey settlement, which still exists, is a continuous line of buildings with a chapel in the middle and, on either side of the chapel, a school—one for boys and the other for girls. The

Asquith boys spent two years at the boys' school, passing their holidays with their mother at Huddersfield. The boys appear to have been quite happy at this school; but this whole arrangement of their lives was brought to an end by the death of their grandfather Willans in 1864.

The family responsibility for the boys then shifted to their uncle, John Willans, who was at that time living in London, at Canonbury. Their mother went for her health to live at St. Leonards-on-Sea, and it was decided that they should live mainly with their uncle. He was married to a daughter of Sir Edward Baines, but had no children. He was at that time a partner in S. W. Silver & Co., and a man of substance. He generously offered to adopt the Asquith boys; but the arrangement stopped short at guardianship. They still continued to spend their holidays with their mother; but John Willans had the main care of them as long as he was in London.

The boys lived with this uncle, John Willans, for nearly three years—from Mr. Asquith's twelfth to his fifteenth year—first in Canonbury, and afterwards at Bickley. Mr. Willans sent them to the City of London School. But at the end of that time Mr. John Willans retired from his London business and became a partner with his brother-in-law, Sir Thomas Freeman Firth, at Lightcliffe, near Brighouse in Yorkshire. It therefore became necessary for him to leave London.

The boys were prospering at the City of London School, and it was considered undesirable to move them again away from London. But there was another maternal uncle living in London— William Henry Willans. He took over the general charge of the nephews from his brother. But it was arranged that they should live as lodgers in the house of Mrs. Barrett in Pimlico. Mrs. Barrett's son was then working with Professor Tyndall at the Royal Institution, and is now Professor Sir William Barrett, of Dublin. Thus early in their lives the two Asquith boys had a glimpse behind the scenes at the miraculous triumphs of modern science.

Here was a strange existence for a future Prime Minister of the British Empire—at fifteen years of age living with his brother, practically uncontrolled, in lodgings in the heart of London, but saved probably from all passing temptations by daily attendance at the City of London School, then domiciled within the City, in Milk Street, Cheapside. The two boys would go to school by penny steamer, would take their midday dinner in a coffee-shop, and would walk home by way of Westminster. The House of Commons then met at four o'clock, and so the young Asquiths, in these daily walks, would pass Downing Street and the House of Commons at that magical hour, so well known to Londoners, when the rulers of this country assemble for their daily duties. Often they would pause in Whitehall or at the entrance to Palace Yard and watch the Ministers and members passing to and fro.* In this way young Asquith grew quite familiar with the faces and names of the leading politicians of that day. It was the moment (1865) when that historic strife between Gladstone and Disraeli was working towards its climacteric; and when that meteoric orator, Mr. Robert Lowe, was beginning to play his brief and brilliant part on the political stage. These were striking figures, gifted with features that held the eye, and young Asquith seemed never to tire of watching them and their movements. It is easy to record prophecies after the event, but those who have the best reason to know have little doubt that even at that time the young Asquith nursed the ambition of being Prime Minister of Great Britain.

* There was at that time a woman stall-owner who sold food in Palace Yard. She kept the boys thoroughly instructed in all the Parliamentary identities. They got to know every face of importance.

BOYHOOD

It is agreed by all who knew him in his youth that Mr. Asquith was marked from the outset by a most rare and remarkable natural endowment in the gift of speech. He began as a young boy of thirteen practising oratory as a parlour sport in his uncle's home at Bickley, and it was always from early days his favourite amusement. In that boyish debating society which, at the City of London, as at other schools, played a considerable part in the training of youth, he spoke frequently and well. It is on record that even at that period he possessed in a form of remarkable maturity all the main features of his subsequent oratorical powers — conciseness, clearness, thoroughness and forcefulness. Dr. Edwin Abbott, the famous Head Master of that school, that distinguished scholar and writer who is happily still among us (1915), gives a remarkable tribute to Mr. Asquith's powers in this respect. Dr. Abbott was in the habit of correcting exercises while he sat in the president's chair of that society; but he has told us that whenever young Asquith spoke he was forced to lay down his exercises to listen. For a head-master that was certainly a remarkable tribute to a pupil's power.

More than twenty years later (1892), when Mr. Asquith was entertained by his school companions on his elevation to the Home Office, he gave to the world a most notable and suggestive comment on the form of existence which he led during these school days :—

"For my part, when I look back upon my old school life, I think not only, and perhaps not so much of hours which I spent in the classroom, or in preparing my lessons at night: I think rather of the daily walk through the crowded, noisy, jostling streets; I think of the river, with its barges and its steamers, and its manifold, active life; I think of St. Paul's Cathedral and Westminster Abbey, and of the National Gallery; I think, even, sometimes of the Houses of Parliament where, I remember, we used occasionally to watch, with a sense of awestruck solemnity, the members disappearing into the inner recesses, which we were not allowed to cross, there to perform the high and mysterious function which their constituents had imposed upon them."

It is certainly a striking commentary on many modern theories of education that Mr. Asquith should have declared at the height of his career that in the retrospect he owed more to the sights of London than to the schoolroom. While admitting that probably it was the inspiration of the schoolroom that gave its value to the impressions gained from Westminster Abbey and St. Paul's Cathedral, we cannot deny that such a verdict delivers a serious blow to any view of education as a mere affair of the cloisters and the refectory.

In any attempt to recover a picture of young Asquith as a boy at school, we have again the immense advantage of the judgments passed by Dr. Edwin Abbott. In all those judgments Dr. Abbott records his impression not so much of a " soaring human boy," but of a great natural force that required very little of the schoolmaster's art for its development. Strength and independence—those seemed to be the qualities which impressed Dr. Abbott most in his wonderful pupil. " From his boyhood upwards," Dr. Abbott said on one occasion, " Mr. Asquith knew what he meant, and knew how to say what he meant." And again, " I never had a pupil that owed less to me and more to his natural ability." Dr. Abbott has also described how he once found young Asquith writing and book-keeping in the fifth form. Instinctively impressed with the inadequacy of that form of training for so remarkable a mind, Dr. Abbott took the boy into his private room and gave him Greek iambics to do while he himself wrote letters. For with this wonderful youth teaching seemed to be almost superfluous. "Simply put the ladder before him," said Dr. Abbott, "and up he went." Thoroughness is perhaps the rarest gift of a brilliant boy. It is often the case, indeed, that a boy pays for his brilliancy by his want of thoroughness. It is the besetting sin of an active, agile mind that it shuns the discipline of toil. But in all these youthful judgments of Mr. Asquith we rarely hear those words—"brilliancy" or "agility." These were not the qualities with which he impressed people. It was then, as now, his thoroughness and sureness that won the world.

Take, for instance, that wonderful gift of speech. It is recorded that in preparing his speeches for the school debating society he always got up his facts most carefully, and mastered his subject before speaking—surely a very rare habit for a schoolboy approaching a debating society. "He had a right to speak his mind," said Dr. Abbott, "because he took so much pains to make it up." That is a verdict not very different from the verdict of the larger public on his later speeches. No wonder that he became Captain of the school, and was easily acknowledged as the leader of his contemporaries.

After some years of this life in Pimlico, their uncle, William Henry Willans, brought them to live nearer him in Islington, where they resided, at first with a Mrs. Mundy, and afterwards, for the last year or two of Mr. Asquith's school life, with the Whittinghams—an old childless couple.

In considering such influences as were brought to bear on Mr. Asquith's youth, we must not forget that he spent his holidays with his mother at St. Leonards. Mrs. Dixon Asquith was a woman of great ability and charm, who maintained all her life a brave and cheerful fight against severe and painful physical disabilities.* It was a happy thing for the boy Asquith that he always had this softer feminine influence as the background of his life. For among all the powers that go to make a boy's character there is still nothing in life stronger than that of a good mother.

There can be no question as to the direction his abilities were taking, even at this early age. He was becoming more and more a scholar—a student of humanity in its widest sense, and of books as the key to humanity—a scholar, historian, a man of affairs. It is better to keep this picture in mind than to build some foolish image of an Admirable Crichton equally efficient on all sides of life. There is a story that Mr. Asquith at a

* Mr. Asquith's mother lived at St. Leonards with her only daughter until the daughter married Mr. Wooding and came to live in London. Mrs. Asquith then lived with the Woodings, and died in their house at the age of sixty.

later period of life made a bicycle of an ingenious kind and showed it to the then Prince of Wales (afterwards Edward VII.), who ordered another of the same kind. There is no truth whatever in that story. Mr. Asquith was never on a bicycle in his life. Among his many and varied powers the gift of mechanics is not to be reckoned. Unlike Mr. Gladstone, he was not an especially keen mathematician in early youth. It is a proof of his great qualities that he has since become so eminent in the realm of finance without any exceptional knowledge of mathematics. This is simply another evidence that finance of the higher kind does not depend so much on mathematics as on statesmanship; and statesmanship is best built upon humanities. That was the training that Mr. Asquith obtained, and it still remains the best known preparation for the government of men.

Not that we must imagine that this boyhood of Mr. Asquith's was all devoted to this sober pursuit of the humanities. It is a common mistake to deny to greatness the gaiety of childhood, or even the spring of youth. It is indeed the defect of London schooling that the boy misses that glorious freedom of the country-side which is within the gift of so many English public schools. Mr. Asquith knew nothing of the playing fields of Eton, or of the swish of the racing oars on the rivers of England. His love of sport came to him later in life, after his schooling days were all over, and it came in the sober and elderly form of golf. But in spite of those losses he was by no means a melancholy or sombre youth. Perhaps it was the gaiety of London—that peculiar gregarious light-heartedness of a crowded capital—that first began to temper the ruggedness of the northern outlook. At any rate the boy Asquith began quite early to go to the theatres; and later on it became his favourite boyish amusement to fight for a place in the first row of the pit in the great London playhouses. It was the day of John Toole and Nellie Farren at the zenith of their fame. John Toole was especially a hero. Henry Irving was still in his apprenticeship and was at that time not too proud to play a second part to John Toole. It was in such a part that Mr. Asquith often saw Irving in those young days.

It was characteristic of the Asquith note of independence that he struck out this theatre line all by himself at a moment when the solitariness of his youth was deepened by the absence of his elder brother. For that boy was at that time invalided from school and London for about a year; and the younger Asquith spent the terms during that period almost alone in London

—nursing, we may imagine, "the unconquerable hope" of ambitious youth. When the elder Asquith returned, it was to find that his younger brother had learnt by heart a whole act of a play called "Dreams" acted at the Gaiety Theatre. From that time forward the boys went to the theatre frequently together.

At the age of seventeen this strange, happy, brotherly, boyish existence came to an end. Mr. Asquith entered for that blue ribbon University distinction, a scholarship at Balliol College, Oxford, and won it. It was the first time that a Balliol scholarship had been won by a boy from the City of London School, and it was a dazzling opening to the great career that lay before the young Asquith. He has himself recorded his feelings on this occasion in language which cannot be improved :—

> "When you are seventeen, when you have no cares, when you have no fears about the future, when you have no compromising past to rise up in judgment against you, the attainment of success is a pure, an unalloyed, an unmitigated satisfaction."

It was with this brilliant flash of joy that the youth stepped from the schoolroom on to the stage of life.

CHAPTER II

UNIVERSITY CAREER (1870–74)

"Not what I have, but what I do is my Kingdom."—
"Sartor Resartus."

MR. ASQUITH went up to Balliol College, Oxford, in the autumn of 1870 as a scholar of the foundation, and stepped into a fraternity of shining youth.

It was a time of intense ferment and activity at that remarkable college, which in the later part of the nineteenth century took at Oxford the place held by Magdalen College in the eighteenth century, and by Oriel in the mid-nineteenth. That active rivalry between the colleges which is most vocal on the river and in the playing fields exists with equal vigour in the realm of the mind; and at this period Balliol College was moving forward to that secular leadership over Oxford thought which it asserted for some twenty years under the illustrious mastership of Dr. Benjamin Jowett.

It is interesting now to look back upon the influence exercised by that remarkable teacher and leader over the many brilliant young men who thronged to his college from all parts of Great Britain.

It was a kind of worldly idealism, preached in lecture-halls and from college pulpits, and supported by a sharp-shooting fire of breakfast-table epigrams and repartees. On Sunday afternoons, from the pulpit in the very modern chapel of the new Balliol, Dr. Jowett poured out to seven generations of Oxford men who had " ears to hear" a gentle, piping, stream of counsel and rebuke, repressing vulgarity and meanness with the one hand, while with the other he refrigerated excessive enthusiasms and moderated extravagant hopes. It was a mingling of worldly warning and unworldly suggestion. We were to be good, but not too good—unselfish, but not selfless—soldier-saints, with lamps trimmed and loins girded for action, but in this world rather than the next. Temporal failure, so he constantly preached, was no test of spiritual success; rather was our righteousness to be judged by our worldly success. Matthew Arnold has expressed the central thought of this teaching in one of his sonnets:—

" he who flagg'd not in the earthly strife,
From strength to strength advancing—only he
His soul well-knit, and all his battles won
Mounts, and that hardly, to eternal life."

UNIVERSITY CAREER (1870-74)

Not a new or a revolutionary doctrine—rather just the old Greek teaching of the " mean," the middle course, applied to modern life—but surprisingly refreshing to the Oxford youth of that period. This rehabilitation of the world came to Oxford after a century of theological strife—after a succession of Evangelicalisms and Puseyisms, of Erastianisms and Tractarianisms— immense diversions of energy from the affairs of this neglected planet. Then, after all this, on the top of all that dilettante playing with monasticisms and mysticisms, came a man who said to the youth of England—" Your work is here and now ! This earth is your garden—till it ! Till it well—become master-gardeners—and great will be your reward ! " It was a reverberating lesson not only to the youth of Oxford, but to England and the world.

Such was the influence which shaped so many of the men who are now foremost in our affairs— not only Mr. Asquith—but perhaps even more potently, Sir Edward Grey, Lord Curzon, Lord Lansdowne, Lord Loreburn, and Lord Milner. Mr. Asquith's was a mind too individual and too independent—already too far matured by a youth of precocious freedom—to have fallen completely subject to any one influence. It was rather the restless, seething, questioning, dialectical life which the Jowett teaching had set going within the college that formed the real stimulus to the growing brain of this remarkable scholar from the City of London.*

There is no more dazzling change in the life of an English boy on the threshold of manhood than this passage from the Spartan discipline of his school life to the Attic freedom of the English University, with its splendid comradeship and equality, its magic mingling of work and leisure. It is a life always touched with the thrill of that wonderful background, the Gothic spires and spreading gardens of the dreaming Middle Ages. These influences—the influences of age and beauty—strike deep; and in later years

* And yet none of Dr. Jowett's pupils has left on record a finer appreciation of his influence than was pronounced by Mr. Asquith on the occasion of Dr. Jowett's death :—
" We cannot hope to see again ever the counterpart of that real and refined intellect in whose presence intellectual lethargy was stirred into life, and intellectual pretentiousness sank into abashed silence. Still less can we hope to see a character such as his—a union of worldly sagacity with the most transparent simplicity of nature ; ambition keen and unsleeping, but entirely detached from self and wholly absorbed in the fortune of a great institution and its members ; generosity on which no call could be too heavy, and a delicate kindliness which made the man himself, always busy in great and exacting studies, always ready to give the best hours either of the day or the night to help and advise the humblest of those who appealed to him for aid. These are the qualities, or some of the qualities, which were the secret of his power, and which are buried in his grave."

those of us who are happy enough to have lived that life find their love of motherland twined round with these memories—unforgettable hours of Oxford spring-time, with its glory of hawthorn and lilac and laburnum—the feel of the water and the hot sun in sheltered bathing-places of the Isis and the Cherwell—the sound of the bells summoning us to worship and work. We too have heard the chimes at midnight. Echoes of these things return, wrapped round with that dominating memory of the environing past, the ever-present sense of the great who have gone before. But never, alas! can we afterwards quite recall those early impressions in the full vigour of their first onset, or realise the power that they exercised in shaping our lives and characters.

It is only some dense covering of idleness or insensibility that can shut the door on these influences; and certainly the young Asquith was neither idle nor insensitive. Industry was always his habit, and plain living was his necessity. The scholars' gown gave him the freedom of the most stimulating society, and the Oxford customs of life—the social breakfast, the midnight talk, the scholar's table—gave him daily occasion for that play of mind which was his peculiar gift. Sir Herbert Warren, the eminent President of Magdalen College, happened to live on the same staircase as Asquith, and he has given us a lively picture of the society that soon began to group round the newcomer.* "The Clique," as it was called, soon began to meet regularly on Saturday evenings for whist and on Sunday mornings for breakfast.

Life at our Universities has not stood still, and there are few forms of English existence which have been more deeply influenced by the great mechanical developments of our times. Nowadays the young men rush to and fro on motor-bicycles and motor-cars; and many of them spend more hours outside the University than inside it. But the seventies were quieter and serener days, when men rode horses and even walked—when in the summer afternoons companions would visit Godstow Bridge or the Cumner Hills, or wander through the Bagley Woods. Now the unrest of modern life has changed much of that—not always for the better. Perhaps thoughts struck deeper into the minds of youth in those days before the telephone bell and the motor-horn. Perhaps men read more widely and wrote better before their minds were distracted by multitudinous impressions from the outer world. At any rate that atmosphere

* In a chapter in Mr. Alderson's "Life of Mr. Asquith" (Methuen & Co.), a book that has helped me much.

seemed to make Oxford life more secluded and detached—a more tranquil nursery for growing minds, a community in itself with its own aims, its own judgments, and its own hero worships.

It was in that society of critical, observant youth that the young Asquith soon began to take a high and illustrious position.

It would be absurd, indeed, to pretend that he instantly stepped into the leadership of his year and generation. These things happen gradually in English University life. It is only afterwards that the fallacy of predestination spreads over the vision, and we see the great man shining in his cradle or moving through life in a ray of discriminating sunshine, a sort of celestial limelight. The "Asquith Year" was afterwards spoken of with bated breath; but it was the last of Mr. Asquith's four years. These distinctions among Englishmen are won in the face of perpetual challenge. A constant process of Saturnalian detraction—a sort of "running of the gauntlet"—is the penalty of greatness in our island, whether at our Universities or afterwards in Parliament. Free criticism is the salt of our public existence.

The young Asquith had to face this experience like every other suitor for fame. He had great contemporaries and active rivals in that boisterous, friendly play of youthful ambition—Alfred Milner, Charles Gore,* Robert Mowbray,† Churton Collins, Thomas Raleigh. Nor must we forget that equally large number of the brilliant whose lamps flicker out from fate or fatigue: for when we are young together there are no shining aureoles to distinguish those who are destined to great places. There is a cheerful equality in such a company; and it is just this equality, this republican concession of equal chances, that dowers our University life with its charm and power, and gives so much influence and authority to an able boy of modest origins. It is the reason why we so often find in England that an able man, coming from the Universities, has already created his following before he steps into the arena of combat.

But however gradual the process, Asquith's influence was certain to extend from the staircase and the college to the other score or so of foundations that make up the life of the University. At first it was the influence of the talker—one of those rare beings, a youth who can talk articulately and clearly, and can fight argument with argument. The rumour of such a talker soon goes round in the life of a university, at any rate

---

* Now Bishop of Oxford.
† Afterwards Sir Robert Mowbray.

among that small group which exists in every college and collectively makes up the intellectual life of the place. It was the rumour of a talker who could achieve victory—a fact of vital importance among the young. For it is not the habit of golden youth to forgive defeat. The life of the mind among the young is always a form of combat, stimulating, exciting, creating. He who wins obtains the biggest following ; and it was always the habit of Mr. Asquith to win—

> " One would aim an arrow fair,
>   But send it slackly from the string ;
> And one would pierce an outer ring,
>   And one an inner, here and there ;
>
> " And last the master-bowman, he
>   Would cleave the mark."

In such youthful contests, hotly fought in the smoke-laden atmosphere of those little college rooms which are more kingly than palaces, it was Mr. Asquith who was the " master-bowman."

But the young Asquith soon discovered a sphere of wider influence. In his power of public speech he was gifted, as we have seen, from early days with a key to unlock the hearts and minds of men. That key he found himself able to apply at Oxford in that notable institution known as the Oxford Union Society. The weekly debates at the " Union " are now a kind of academic understudy to Parliament in modern Oxford life ; and it is a commonplace to describe that lofty seated hall, with its air of a mimic House of Commons, as a nursery of British oratory. But there have been times when the influence of the Oxford Union has waned and seemed about to die out. It is only the sustained efforts of a succession of public-spirited undergraduates that have kept alive the spirit of this remarkable society. Among these undergraduates, Mr. Asquith acquired a leading place.

In reviving the Union and restoring it to the place which, with occasional ups and downs, it has held ever since in Oxford life, Asquith and his group performed a great service. For although there are some young minds and young ideas which bloom better in the hot-house seclusion of those smaller speculative clubs which always abound in a University, yet it is in the life of a central society that the true University spirit must always be best expressed. The life of a mediæval University found its daily expression in open discussion on all themes human and divine; and in an age where the printed and written word threatens to extinguish speech, these great centres of open dialectical combat provide a wholesome and useful corrective. There—in these debates—is the breath of the open sea: there the wind blows freely. There is the place for the man who is willing to hang out his banner on the outer wall. The young Asquith was just such a man; and this training-ground precisely suited his temperament.

Contemporaries tell us that Mr. Asquith spoke then almost as well as he does now. This seems almost as difficult to believe as that old story with which our schoolmasters tested our youthful powers of faith—that Minerva sprang fully armed from the head of Jove. But there are many witnesses still alive; and we must accept their evidence. His voice was, of course, less powerful; for it is the practice of speaking that develops the power of the voice. But he had then the same gift of order, the same inevitable, effortless clearness in phrase and expression, the same merciful brevity and conciseness. We can imagine the effect produced by these great gifts over an audience of young men. For he was then, as now, coolly prepared for any interruption; and that alone must have been a tremendous advantage with an audience that delights to trip and disturb—almost mischievously intent to dispute the will to prevail. There are Parliamentarians of much experience in debate at Westminster who are wont to declare that the Oxford Union Society was to them a more difficult place of debate than the House of Commons; and bold will he be who, at any age, faces unprepared that amphitheatre of merciless, mocking youth.

Here lies precisely the value of the Union to the young speaker in search of a training—that it possesses all the inclemency of the larger world. Every speaker must submit his faith to bold and brawling challenge. Those who survive such an ordeal by fire have little to fear in after life from the ribaldry of mobs or the insolence of elected persons.

Mr. Asquith throve in that atmosphere, and soon moved steadily towards leadership. He was in those days, as ever since, a thorough-going party-man, and he had to endure the vicissitudes of party struggle. He was defeated in his first contest for the Presidency by Ellis Ashmead Bartlett,* and had to wait a year for that crown. In this way he learned in early life the true secret of political life, to take, without swerving or shrinking, the rough with the smooth, the shower with the shine, the defeat with the victory—to join those who, like Ulysses of old,

> ". . . ever with a frolic welcome took
> The thunder and the sunshine;"

and if that lesson has stood him in good stead through life, he probably learnt it first in these youthful combats at the Oxford Union.

It would be foolish and unjust to exaggerate

* Afterwards Sir Ellis Ashmead Bartlett, M.P.

the importance of the opinions expressed in these youthful jousts of the mind—to rummage in the records of the Union Society for startling and disconcerting expressions of the young Asquith. But it is worth while to note one or two resolutions which he moved in those far-off days of 1870-71. He opposed the retention of the Bishops in the House of Lords. He moved a resolution of his own in opposition to intervention on behalf of France in the Franco-German War. In 1871 he supported the separation of the Church and State. In 1872 he sustained the surprising proposition—carried by two votes in November —" that the disintegration of the Empire is the true solution of the Colonial difficulty." In a notable debate he opposed Milner, Hyndman, and Lyttelton Gell on a motion on behalf of Imperial Federation. Without attaching too much importance to the growing pains of youthful speculation, it is clear that Mr. Asquith then belonged to that left wing of the Liberal party which is often described by the term " Radical." He had carried on the severe tradition of his Nonconformist ancestry and stood especially for a Free Church in a Free State.* In his attitude

* Mr. Asquith is recorded in 1870 to have taken the place of an absent proposer, and moved a resolution in favour of the principle of compulsion in the Army. This was probably a youthful piece of paradoxical daring.

towards the Colonies and the Empire, he clearly in those days followed the school of Cobden and Bright.

But it was not so much what he advocated. It was the way he advocated it—the new style and tradition of debate which he introduced, and which lasted long after his time. The prevailing impression then, as now, was of finish and perfection. "Cool and courageous," says Sir Herbert Warren, our excellent witness, "intellectually alert, well-informed, sure of himself, with a voice clear and sufficiently strong and flexible, if not specially powerful, and a striking command of apt and incisive language, he was ready for any emergency." That description, almost in every phrase, might be applied with almost equal accuracy to Mr. Asquith to-day. In speech as in talk, Mr. Asquith was from the first the "Master Bowman." The general impression of these youthful speeches was summed up by his contemporaries in one of those couplets which our young barbarians love—

"See Asquith soon in Senates to be first
If Age shall ripen what his youth rehearsed."

It is characteristic of the mature sobriety which marked the young Asquith from the first that his efforts in debate did not at any time cause him to neglect the labour of the schools. Probably the excitements of the Union drew off some strength; but nevertheless he advanced from triumph to triumph with steady strides. He soon began to be spoken of in that confidential argot of the common-room as " the most promising man of his year," and it was expected that he would go far. New stars are always arising in that moving firmament of the University; and it is part of the frank generosity of that society that their rising is almost always welcomed. Asquith's triumphs were always popular. In the two great examinations of the classical scholar— " Moderations " and " Greats "—he was placed in the illustrious circle of the " Firsts," the only human stratification known to the stern Oxford traditions. In 1872 he was posted as " Proxime Accessit " to the Hertford scholarship. In 1873 he was honourably mentioned for the Ireland; and in 1874 he so nearly won it that he was given a prize of books as a proof of prowess. It was after these experiences that he is recorded to have said to Milner, with a flash of that dry humour which now assuages the wrath of Parliaments— " We have both known what it is to ' approximate.' "

But in the following years he knew also what it was to arrive. He won that glittering prize of the graduate, the Craven scholarship, and—greater honour still—he was admitted into the Fellowship of Balliol College. It can be truly said of him that only two other Asquiths have eclipsed his academic record, and those are his own sons, Raymond and Cyril.

Mr. Asquith's University life was practically over in 1874, and in spite of obtaining the Balliol Fellowship he does not appear ever to have contemplated the devotion of his life to University teaching. There is a well-known story that a Balliol man, addressing Dr. Jowett with that manner of approaching an oracle not uncommon among his pupils, put to the great man this question, " Will Asquith get on ? " To which Dr. Jowett replied, with that Johnsonian brevity of his, " Yes, he will get on ; he is so direct." That puts in a terse form one verdict on Mr. Asquith's character at the moment when he emerged from his Oxford training. Like so many things said of Mr. Asquith at that period, it is as true of him to-day as it was then. In 1915, as in 1874, Mr. Asquith gets on because he is so direct. Every quality has its own defect, and it was perhaps a true perception which suggested to another Oxford critic the remark, " Asquith has no uncalculating idealism." But what is true of Mr. Asquith in that respect is equally true of the British people, and it is gravely to be doubted whether "uncalculating" idealism should be regarded as a merit in one who aspires to mould this nation. At any rate it is quite certain that the British people regard such idealism with peculiar suspicion, and perhaps it is Mr. Asquith's very lack of it—his intense practicality—that is the secret of his power over the British race.

So now at the age of twenty-two we see him leaving the garden-city of Oxford—that secluded paradise of fortunate youth—for a wider, rougher, sterner sphere. We see him going out fully equipped with every weapon in the armoury of bold debate, intent upon greater combats and larger victories. It was certainly better so; for it was already clear that this young man possessed powers of a robuster kind than were needed for the shielded strifes of academic life.

CHAPTER III

FROM COLLEGE TO PARLIAMENT

"Men at some time are masters of their fates."—
Julius Caesar.

THERE is no more critical moment in any young man's career than when he steps out from his University demesne on to the unsheltered battle-ground of the outer world. He will probably be faced on the threshold with some arresting reminders of his own insignificance.

For at Oxford the undergraduate is practically an aristocrat, waited on by a large community mostly devoted to his services. It is a small world of its own. Within that self-contained sphere, a man of brains and capacity may become a little god to his own generation; and in the self-confidence of youth he may be tempted to imagine that he is a god indeed.

But outside that sacred fence, he will soon discover that London is not Oxford. For that great stormy, cheerful, boisterous voice of the capital is always inclined to challenge and dispute the verdict of the universities.

FROM COLLEGE TO PARLIAMENT 35

It is the shock of this discovery which is often the chief crisis in a young man's career : for it comes as a chill to all his firmest beliefs, and makes a call upon energies which are often already fatigued. It applies a new test to a man's brains and character.

But the young Asquith knew his outer world already : and this change, therefore, came with less effect. The freedom of that early London upbringing had given him a fund of self-reliance not easily to be exhausted. His Balliol Fellowship, too, softened the blow, and gave him resources for a period of rest before launching his vessel on to the outer seas. He did not stay at Oxford for long after taking his degree. Very soon after, he became tutor to the young Lord Lymington, the heir to the Wallop family, the present Lord Portsmouth.*

This experience of private tutoring to the scion of a noble house is not rare among the picked men of the Universities, who are thus called upon to reinforce birth with brains. In Mr. Asquith's case it was not destined to last long. After only six months of private teaching he went to London.

There he entered at Lincoln's Inn, like so

* Since that period a Liberal member of Parliament (1880–86). A Liberal-Unionist member (1886–91), and once more Liberal Under-Secretary for War (1905–8), and Ecclesiastical Commissioner (1909).

many young Oxford men in his position, at this stage of the great career; and he began those studies of Roman and other law which are laid down as necessary for an English lawgiver. He passed rapidly through the easy examinations which form the entrance-gate to this calling. He was called to the Bar in 1876, and began to sit daily in chambers within the Temple.

But meanwhile the young Asquith was already looking round for other outlets for his expanding energies; and perhaps the prospect of marriage played some part in this search. The first beginnings of a young barrister's career are notoriously as unprofitable as they are laborious; and there is no profession which follows more literally the stern scriptural rule of giving only to those who already possess. Mr. Asquith looked round for other means of livelihood, and he found them like so many other gifted young men, in the exercise of the pen and the voice. The voice was always his more finished gift, and during these years, being free for the moment from political calls, he devoted himself strenuously to the work of lecturing. Mr. Asquith was one of the first lecturers of the University Extension Movement in London. That movement was then trying its first tottering steps in the great teeming metropolis, amid the indifference and ridicule of men. It required daring and sympathy to take up this flickering torch and carry it forward. Mr. Asquith, with his supreme gift of clear and easy speech, was the very man for the task. He lectured for several years in many parts of London, but especially in Wimbledon, and he became a successful and popular lecturer.

Sixteen years later, at a meeting of the London University Extension Society in the days of its established pride, he told the story of these early struggles. He confided to his audience the anxieties and uncertainties of those early days. Those were times, he said, when courses of lectures had to be suspended for lack of supporters. Oxford and Cambridge were very cold towards the movement in those days; grey-haired dons shook stiff, elderly heads and talked about " coming down to the people," and the danger of democracy to learning. The young Asquith was never frightened of those dangers. Economics formed his principal theme; and it was by the processes of study and thought necessary for these lectures that he acquired that rare and striking mastery of the Free Trade argument which, some thirty years later, proved so surprising and disconcerting to Mr. Joseph Chamberlain.

This effort to carry the spirit of University teaching, with all its breadth and depth, into the highways and byways of this great seething modern England was certainly one of the most remarkable of the many educational developments that marked the close of the nineteenth century. No one who took part in that movement can forget the extraordinary stir and ferment of those pioneer days—the crowded audiences of eager artisans filling the town halls, the little groups of artisans and teachers that gathered together in the village schools, or even the inspired garden-parties and tea-parties that thronged into the vicarage drawing-rooms and gardens. They came to listen to some youthful missioner from Oxford or Cambridge in the same spirit with which in the Middle Ages men and women came to listen to some Abelard or Paracelsus. There was the same thrill—the same eager sense of a new illumination.

Do not let us talk lightly of that movement. It was in spirit the same as that which nearly a thousand years before, spread the seeds of learning over Europe and led to the foundation of the Oxford and Cambridge Universities themselves.*

The task of lecturing for the Extension was a wonderful school of training for the young men

---

* The Extension movement has already led to the foundation of several Colleges, as for instance Reading and Exeter.

who undertook it. It gave them a wide and varied experience in speaking to men and women in every class of English society. It made them experts in the art of making the steep places level and the crooked paths straight. The Extension lecturer had an audience and a subject. He was compelled to be a student as well as a speaker. His work gave him sympathy and understanding for the poor in substance and station, and a daily insight into their struggle and yearnings. There could be no better preparation for the better side of public life.

Thus while Oxford taught Mr. Asquith quickness, London taught him sympathy. The London lecturer's platform came to supplement and complete the training of the Oxford Union Society.

But Mr. Asquith allowed none of these wayside activities to draw him off from that steady, day-to-day application which is the necessary condition of success at the Bar. He avoided that enforced leisure which falls like a Mephistophelean shadow, dark with temptations to ease, across the young barrister's path. The lecturer of the evening before often found it easier to spend a day waiting in Chambers; and thus other occupations took off the edge of that heavy tedium which besets the youth of England at the Inns of the law. Mr. Asquith was wise enough to know that patience was allotted as the badge of his new calling, patience at youth's most impatient hour, rest for the active, tide-waiting for the young, restless mariner. It is a hard, testing experience; and in that race of the tortoise and the hare the first often become the last.

But Mr. Asquith had already a wise head on young shoulders; and he steadily stuck to the course set before him, in spite of that discouragement which has so often driven less hardy pursuers from the quest.

Briefs were scarce at first. Success at the Bar did not come to Mr. Asquith rapidly or easily. We are conscious that during those ten years (from 1874 to 1884) Mr. Asquith's career takes a pause like that of a river approaching rapids. The current goes deeper. During such pauses it often happens that the vital energies are accumulating for larger and bolder efforts. Perhaps the astonishing physical and mental robustness of Mr. Asquith in later life may be traced to these ten years of steady leisurely work and happy, industrious existence, sweetened by domestic life.

For in 1877, when he was twenty-five years of age, Mr. Asquith married, after an engagement of less than two years, Miss Helen Melland, the daughter of Dr. Frederick Melland of Manchester.

FROM COLLEGE TO PARLIAMENT 41

This young wife of his youth was a woman of that type of sweet, self-less charm which Coventry Patmore has described for all time in " The Angel in the House." Those women of the mid-nineteenth century, the mother of the men now in middle life, were perhaps the noblest product of that Victorian England of our youth. They represented one of those moments in human development when some human type seems to reach a perfect symmetry, a fine, flawless balance of emotion and temperament.

Of such women Miss Melland was a noble example—domestic, unambitious, sweet in expression, sweet in nature :

> " A perfect woman, nobly planned,
> To warn, to comfort, and command ;
> And yet a Spirit still, and bright
> With something of angelic light."

The young couple went to live at Hampstead, in a street then known as John Street, now re-baptised as Keats's Grove, from the fact that Keats lived there when he wrote his " Ode to the Nightingale," and sang of the—

> " White hawthorn, and the pastoral eglantine ;
> Fast fading violets cover'd up in leaves ;
> And mid-May's eldest child,
> The coming musk-rose, full of dewy wine,
> The murmurous haunt of flies on summer eves."

Hampstead has changed since such sights were

seen and such sounds heard; and it was rather in what was already a London suburb—though always the best of London suburbs—that the Asquiths set up a modest household, each bringing some help to the common income. The young husband went daily to Lincoln's Inn, studied for his lectures, and wrote for the newspapers. The great Lord Salisbury, at a similar period, wrote for the *Saturday Review*. Mr. Asquith wrote for *The Spectator* and the *Economist*.

The children began to come; and in those years were born those splendid sons [*] who have already carried on the light of Mr. Asquith's name in the schools and on the battlefield. Mr. Asquith had to work harder; for although the filling of the quiver enables us to speak with our enemies in the gate, it also brings upon us new demands which may, unless promptly met, become enemies also.

But after all, these little new-comers form the best inspiration for work, and with excellent reasons for activity Mr. Asquith began to move steadily forward in his profession. Whatever he did he did well; and in that most critical

---

[*] Raymond, Herbert, Arthur, and Cyril. Arthur and Herbert have both been wounded in battle. The other member of his first family is Miss Violet Asquith, now engaged to Mr. Asquith's secretary, Mr. Bonham Carter. His second family consists of Miss Elizabeth and Master Anthony Asquith.

FROM COLLEGE TO PARLIAMENT 43

of all the professions, a reputation for sound, steady workmanship is perhaps the best basis for success. It is the solicitors who administer favours to the young barristers; and the solicitors of England do not pursue brilliancy for its own sake. What they chiefly want is success. But they will forgive even failure if it is redeemed by industry, or by persistence that forecasts success in the future.

Like many young barristers with an interest in politics, Mr. Asquith displayed a liking for social or political cases. Thus he appeared in that famous case when the Anti-Gambling League made its formidable effort to destroy the whole industry and pursuit of betting as attached to the sport of horse-racing, by appealing to the Bench to declare that the betting-ring was a " place " of the kind forbidden to betting under the Act which restricts gambling in these islands. In this notable case, the anti-gamblers failed in their daring blow at a national weakness patronised by the great. But Mr. Asquith put up a very good fight. It was in the course of a skirmish with the judge that Mr. Asquith perpetrated an excellent repartee. " Suppose," said Mr. Justice Wright, " that I were to give you an area marked with the meridians of longitude, would that constitute a place in your opinion ? "

To which Mr. Asquith replied with equal wit and sense, " That, my Lord, would be merely a matter of degree."

His next case of a kind affecting public affairs was when in 1886 he defended Mr. John Burns and Mr. Cunninghame Graham for breaking through a cordon of police in their attempt to hold a meeting in Trafalgar Square, then a forbidden place for public speech. Both Mr. Burns and Mr. Graham were sent to prison; but it was undoubtedly as a result of their action that the Square was thrown open to meetings by Mr. Asquith himself in 1892, and has been open for that purpose ever since.

It was a later political trial that, after many years, gave Mr. Asquith his first brilliant success, and sufficiently established his name at the Bar to justify him in taking silk in 1890.

Mr. Asquith had been chosen in 1889 by Sir Charles Russell to act as his junior in the defence of Mr. Parnell and his fellow-members before the Royal Commission of Judges appointed to inquire into the notorious charges of the *Times* newspaper contained in that historic brochure, " Parnellism and Crime." One day at the luncheon hour Sir Charles Russell was fatigued with his work, and, turning to Mr. Asquith, he said, " Take my next witness." The witness

FROM COLLEGE TO PARLIAMENT 45

happened to be James MacDonald, the manager of the *Times* newspaper, and Mr. Asquith pointed out the great importance of his examination. But in such a case the great advocate was apt to be self-willed. "I am tired," said Russell, "and you will do it well enough." The result was the examination of the *Times* manager by Mr. Asquith. It was the examination which exposed the forgery of Pigott, and was perhaps the most sensational success of the whole trial. It has been described as "one of the most brilliant and skilful displays of word-baiting ever witnessed in a court of law." When Mr. Asquith sat down his reputation was made. He had taken his place among that small group of lawyers who are wont to share all the glory and most of the profits in that great and splendid profession. By the merest "accident of an accident," as he himself has phrased it, Mr. Asquith had seized fame with both hands and had plucked in a moment the fruits of all his labours during the previous ten years.

Three years before this notable success, but not unrelated to it, had come an equally conspicuous victory in another field. Mr. Asquith had won a seat in Parliament at the General Election of 1886.

This sounds an easy statement in retrospect;

but we must not imagine that all the gates to Parliament opened, or that all the roads grew straight, at Mr. Asquith's approach. There are moments in the lives of men which make a sudden call on the power of personal judgment, and at such turning points the wisest often go astray. It was such a moment that came to Mr. Asquith in 1886, when the defeat of Mr. Gladstone's first Home Rule Bill split the Liberal party, fresh from its victory in 1885, and forced upon the country a confused and divided conflict. Far away up in Scotland, in the East Fife Division, Mr. Boyd Kinnear, a Liberal member of Parliament of high standing, with a strong hold upon the confidence of his constituency, had thrown off his allegiance to Mr. Gladstone and decided to fight the seat as a Liberal-Unionist. It looked as if the seat was certainly lost; and there were weak-kneed counsellors who were in favour of allowing Mr. Kinnear a walk-over. But on June 26, 1886, those sturdy Scotchmen, the Liberals and Radicals of East Fife, voted by 53 to 7 that "Mr. Kinnear was an unfit person to represent Liberalism in Parliament," and proceeded to call upon Mr. Asquith to stand in his place.

The enterprise did not appear very hopeful. Mr. Asquith had indeed refused several offers of Parliamentary candidature. But he was still

FROM COLLEGE TO PARLIAMENT 47

little known in political life. He was a complete stranger to East Fife, and had only a week to fight the seat. Mr. Kinnear was a popular and well-known man in the constituency, and was supported not merely with the whole force of the Tory party, but by many powerful Dissentient Liberals. No wonder that many shrewd advisers strongly counselled Mr. Asquith to refuse the invitation of the East Fife Gladstonians.

Mr. Asquith has been known to say that all the most important steps in his life have been taken against the advice of his elders; and in this case there seemed everything to be said for these counsels of caution and discretion which have ruined so many bright lives. But Mr. Asquith never hesitated. He accepted the invitation.

Mr. Asquith went to Fife: he saw; he conquered. In a brief and brilliant campaign, fighting manfully and confidently against heavy odds, he wrenched this seat from its former member; and in the midst of the gloom of that disastrous time came to Westminster as one of the rare victors in the cause of Gladstonian Home Rule.*

Thus he now placed a foot on the first rung of that ladder which was to take him up to the highest place in the British Empire.

* Mr. Asquith won the seat by 374. The figures were—Asquith, 2863; Boyd Kinnear, Liberal-Unionist, 2489.

CHAPTER IV

PARLIAMENT

"A Life in civic action warm,
   A soul on highest mission sent,
   A potent voice in Parliament,
A pillar steadfast in the storm."
        TENNYSON, "In Memoriam" canto 113.

WHEN Mr. Asquith entered the House of Commons in 1886 the Liberal cause in Great Britain appeared to have sustained a calamity greater than ever before in the nineteenth century.

For the defeat of the first Home Rule Bill in the House of Commons on June 8 had been followed by a General Election which resulted in a complete reversal of the Liberal victory in 1885. The supporters of the Act of Union returned to Parliament with a majority of 110 over all Home Rulers —English, Scotch, and Irish.* The Liberal

---

* The British Liberals were reduced from 235 to 196. The Tories rose from 251 to 316. The Liberal Unionists fell to 74, and the Irish Nationalists under Mr. Parnell came back in the same strength.

Cabinet instantly resigned, and the Tories, on August 3, formed a strong and confident Ministry, intent upon giving the final dispatch to the whole policy of Home Rule. The twenty years of " resolute government " prophesied by Lord Salisbury, were now to begin.

It was written, indeed, in the book of fate that England, rather than Ireland, was to suffer by the great refusal of 1886. While the peace of Ireland was, in the end, to be won rather by concession than by coercion, England was to pay for her obstinacy by twenty years of reaction.

Mr. Asquith's Parliamentary career is part of the great story of the resistance to that great reaction carried on by a small group of brilliant men, differing on many subjects, but agreed in their resolution not to abate one jot of their faith in the cleansing and redeeming virtues of liberty, tolerance, and self-government. It was they who kept alight the flame of freedom, and saved the Liberal party in England from the eclipse which blotted it out in Germany.

For the moment, indeed, the great defeat was Mr. Asquith's opportunity. In the very blackness of the night Mr. Asquith's star shone more brightly. He had saved a seat, and he came to Westminster as a welcome recruit to a cause in jeopardy—a recruit already famous for clear speech, straight thought, and stalwart principle. He had the advantage of that strange law which turns the misfortune of the whole into the gain of the individual. For when his party is in power the private member is little better than a slave. He is gagged and throttled by the Whips. He is encouraged to a life of a silent perambulation. Any act of independence is accounted an act of rebellion. In Opposition, on the contrary, all this is changed. The private member is stimulated to every form of parliamentary piracy. He is taught to regard independence a merit and recklessness as a shining virtue. The rebellions of yesterday become the loyalties of to-day. Indiscretion becomes an art. To become a nuisance is the end of existence for the opposition member who aims at success. If he impede business, well and good. If he embarrass the Government, all the better. If he should upset it entirely, best of all.

Mr. Asquith was not fashioned after that gay and adventurous kind that suck the most dazzling advantage from such a situation. It was not his nature to greet the thunder with a " frolic welcome." Perhaps he had before him the tremendous warning of Lord Randolph Churchill, whose giddy rise to power, and equally rapid fall, was the daily drama of Mr. Asquith's early parliamentary years. Such swift gains and losses are the very food of the adventurous nature. There are those, indeed, who even on the balance would prefer to a slower advance such glorious hours of crowded life, however brief and few. But Mr. Asquith was never an adventurer. Neither in youth nor in age has he ever been in love with giddiness. He has never lacked daring. But he has always preferred the steady march along the high-road to the dizzy scramble up the rocks. Caution was ever the mortar of his character; and if caution failed there was always a certain element of shyness which saved him from excess of risk. For the life of a poor young man who is making his own way in English public affairs, without birth or fortune behind him, is always lived upon a perilous razor-edge of danger. There is always, in case of a slip, a black gulf of disaster yawning for him on either side.

Mr. Asquith had to win his laurels afresh. For an Oxford reputation rarely extends beyond a comparatively small circle unless immediately followed up by success in the larger world. The lapse of ten years had now left that star of fame rather dim and misty, even with his own University generation. There was even, in some quarters, a feeling of disappointment that he had not yet justified the splendid hero worship of the colleges.

He had, indeed, been elected in 1883 to that new and vigorous combination of young Liberals, founded in 1880, to celebrate the great victory of that year—the " Eighty Club." In 1884 he had seconded Mr. Alfred Lyttleton in a vote of thanks to John Bright at a dinner given to that mighty veteran. In 1885 he had been elected to the committee of the club at the very moment when Mr. Gladstone was chosen for a presidency which he held until his death. These were first steps. But considering his earlier successes it cannot be said that he had yet achieved anything in politics worthy of his early reputation. He entered Parliament practically as a new man.

The Unionist Parliament assembled in the autumn of 1886; but it was not until March 24, 1887, after some months of silence, that Mr. Asquith made his maiden speech. The occasion was the debate on the Crimes Bill—the " coercion for ever and ever Bill," as it was called by its critics. For though Ireland had known since the Act of Union nearly a hundred Coercion Acts, this was the first time that coercion had been made part of the permanent law of the land. It was a characteristic piece of daring on the part of that little band of aristocrats who had now grasped the reins of government, that they accepted freely and boldly Mr. Gladstone's dialectical challenge. They agreed with him that the only alternative to Home Rule was to be found in repression. Thus gaily at the close of the nineteenth century, a British Government entered upon the experiment of creating a second Poland.

It was that new departure which Mr. Asquith clearly put before the House of Commons in his first speech.

The speech is a plain, straight, courageous, political utterance, independent but not eccentric, brave but not reckless, pleasing to friends and yet not offensive to enemies—just such a first utterance as the House of Commons loves. Law and liberty—these were the two guiding principles, and between them Mr. Asquith steered his steady middle course, opposing with equal steadiness repression on the one side and lawlessness on the other.[*]

But it is clearly not what Mr. Asquith said so much as the way in which he said it that impressed the House of Commons. The speech was given one and a half columns in the *Times* on the following

---

[*] As for instance: " In his judgment, it was the duty of the Executive not to inquire whether the law was good or bad, just or unjust, but to enforce it in all places, at all times, without distinction of persons, without discrimination of cases, with undeviating uniformity, with irresistible strength " (Hansard, Vol. 312, 1394).

day, and Hansard reported it fairly, although not in the first person. But the most notable sign of the moment was the greeting which Mr. Asquith received from Mr. Chamberlain, who followed him in debate. Mr. Chamberlain was not always marked by kindness to new-comers in the House of Commons, and that fact made his greeting all the more remarkable. "All who listened," he said, "will agree with me that the speech is a favourable augury of the position which Mr. Asquith is likely to fill in our parliamentary contests." A notable greeting, already phrased as from equal to equal.

Mr. Asquith stepped on to the stage, of course, fully equipped for the contest. The youthful experiences of the school debating society and the Oxford Union had now been nourished and ripened by the Extension platform and the work in the Law Courts. Already at thirty-five, Mr. Asquith had had a large and varied experience of many forms of speaking; and his chief temptation now must have been not so much the usual fear and hesitation of the beginner, as the perilous fluency and ease of the expert. If he had been restless and importunate for success his great gifts might easily have been only a preparation for failure. For that amazingly sensitive audience of the House of Commons resents nothing so much as familiarity and frequency of address in those who would seek its favours. Many a speaker, scarcely less brilliant than Mr. Asquith, has come to disaster in his wooing owing to a want of the sense of fitness in time and opportunity.

"There is a time for speech and a time for silence," says the ancient sage ; Mr. Asquith's great achievement as a young parliamentarian was that he knew the time for silence as well as the time for speech.

The rarity of his speeches was certainly not due to the want of encouragement. For his victory at the polls and the excellence of his maiden speech soon made him a popular figure in the party, and he was much sought after in public functions. On April 18, of this year, 1887, he was chosen to occupy the chair at a famous dinner of good cheer and good-will given by the " Eighty Club " to Mr. Gladstone. It is still a tradition in the Club that Mr. Gladstone was enormously impressed by Mr. Asquith's speech and conversation ; and from that time forward Mr. Gladstone held in his retentive memory a clear impression and conviction of Mr. Asquith's character and ability.

Later in the year (October 18) Mr. Asquith was again chosen as a " star " speaker—this time on behalf of a Home Rule resolution at the meeting of the National Liberal Federation—that strange, stormy, annual assembly of the party which gives a passionate expression to the wishes and favours of the Liberal rank and file. "An eloquent and powerful speech," said Mr. Morley; and the very fact of Mr. Asquith's selection for this task marked his steady rise in favour with the great Liberal public throughout the country.

But Mr. Asquith did not allow his head to be turned by any of these compliments. It was in the House of Commons that the laurels had to be plucked, and there a careless or a hasty hand might easily tear or rend the bay leaves before he placed them on his brow. He moved forward with a deliberation that seemed almost too cold for his admirers. Looking through the Hansard of that time we find extraordinary few utterances for one who was so soon destined for parliamentary eminence. When he does speak it is almost always on that question of Irish Home Rule which had been the occasion of his entrance into political life.

During the following years there raged that great controversy over the conduct of the Irish revolt against English rule which now seems to us so remote, but at that time an acutely divided thought and opinion. It was a kind of " Atrocity agitation " against the Irish leaders, organised by men doubtless sincere, but with judgment distorted by racial and religious passion. The promoters of this movement hoped to deliver a final blow to the Irish party, and dreamed of the exclusion of Parnell's most brilliant followers from public life. They had great resources, and they had on their side the potent engine of a great newspaper—none other than the *Times*. It was in the columns of the *Times* that they threw out their startling gage of battle in the facsimile of the Parnell letter to the " Invincible " murderers

It was to clear up the truth of this terrific charge that the Parnell Commission was created by the Unionist Government in 1888.

Throughout every twist and turn of this bitter controversy, Mr. Asquith played an active part. It was practically the only question that he spoke on in the House ; and after his sensational success before the Commission itself, his speeches carried immense weight.

Here was already evidence of that intense power of concentration which Mr. Asquith always brought to bear on his political work. From the beginning he has never spoken unless he had something to say.

Meanwhile he was steadily making himself better known in that large outer world which politicians call the " country." While he baulked and puzzled his admirers at Westminster by his silence, he was a ready worker in those wider fields which are often whitening to harvest while the labourers are still few. Perhaps Mr. Asquith, with his broad outlook on modern government, had already grasped the fact that the secret of the future in politics is generally to be found not in London, but in the provinces.

It is not until 1890 that we find the usual short paragraph allotted to second-rank politicians by the *Times* newspaper expanding to that significant half-column which means that the halo of coming greatness is already shining on the brow. During these years—from 1888 to 1892—he spoke in most of the Northern towns, and won from places like Leeds and Manchester that sturdy approval which is just as important to public men as the smile of London.

Gradually, in these speeches, we begin to detect that note of common-sense independence which has ever since been the hall-mark of Mr. Asquith's influence. Take this question of Irish Home Rule, then the supreme touchstone of British politics. It was on the Home Rule issue that Mr. Asquith came into politics, and ever since, through all the vicissitudes of that great debate, he has remained true to his original faith. But perhaps because he is also an Imperialist he has always recognised the immense electioneering difficulty of persuading one people to allow another to escape from its own control; and he has never suspended his freedom of judgment as to the means and measures to be taken for a final settlement. At that moment, watching that amazing "Grand Old Man" struggling heroically forward in the last desperate fight of his life, Mr. Asquith retained a certain cool aloofness of judgment in regard to the tactics of the campaign. He was of opinion that Mr. Gladstone would have done well to have spent some part of these seven years of delay—1886 to 1892—in solving some of those great unsettled problems which remained over from the discussions of 1886. Mr. Gladstone doubtless saw the danger of presenting his remorseless opponents with a new opportunity of dividing his ranks. But the actual issue of 1893 confirmed Mr. Asquith's fears. For at that crisis of his fate, Mr. Gladstone was seriously weakened by his indecision on certain vital questions—such as the Irish representation at Westminster.

From 1890 onwards Mr. Asquith pressed steadily on Mr. Gladstone the desirability of giving to the country a "broad and general outline" of his proposals. There is a class of political wire-pullers who stoutly believe that the only true way to govern a democracy is to keep them in ignorance of your designs. Doubtless those clever gentry were very angry with Mr. Asquith. But Mr. Gladstone himself certainly bore him no grudge for his frankness, and the British people have since learned to regard this habit of frank dealing as one of Mr. Asquith's greatest qualities.

Mr. Gladstone was probably all the more ready to forgive Mr. Asquith because, among all his lieutenants in that last battle, he had no more resolute champion than Mr. Asquith. The Home Ruler of those days had no easy time. He was often boycotted in society and penalised in his profession. He would be genially told that he was a " friend of assassins " and the " enemy of his country." But Mr. Asquith was not a man to be affected by such amenities. He stood steadily to his guns, not only through the storms of the Parnell Commission, but, what was far worse, through the bitter and perilous disillusionment of the Parnell divorce case. He boldly stated that if all the charges against the Nationalists had been proved true he would still have remained a Home Ruler ; * and, in the crash of Parnell's downfall he refused to recognise that the fault of one man could be the death warrant of a nation.† In this way he built up, during these years, a great reputation for courage as a public man.

* February 26, 1890, at the Belmont Hall, Clapham.
† January 9, 1891, Manchester Reform Club.

All this time he was making steady progress at the Bar; and in 1890 he deemed it safe to "take silk." From 1889 onward, indeed—after the Macdonald cross-examination—his position as a barrister was achieved. But it may console aspiring young men to know that this success was not attained without a severe struggle. Speaking many years after (1909) Mr. Asquith gave a vivid and human description of his early years at the Bar—the little rooms in Fig-tree Court; the help he was glad enough to take from Bowen and James; * his great joy over a guinea County Court brief. His first professional step forward came when he was taken into the chambers of Mr. Wright—afterwards Mr. Justice Wright— who gave him great experience in railway cases. Being at the Common Law Bar, Asquith's chief work during these years was with juries; but he did not really begin to achieve eminence until he appeared before higher tribunals, such as the Parnell Commission, the Railway Commission, and, later, the Privy Council. In proportion as he rose in the scale of tribunals his success increased. When he pleaded before that Appeal

* Lord Bowen, the famous Lord of Appeal, who was also a Fellow of Balliol, and Sir Henry James, afterwards Lord James of Hereford, who refused Mr. Gladstone's offer of the Lord Chancellorship on account of his conscientious objections to the Home Rule policy.

Court which is known as "the House of Lords" he became famous for his effective replies, and there was a time before the Privy Council when he practically shared the business with the friend who is now Lord Haldane. It was in connection with his Bar work that Mr. Asquith wrote his only book. He called it an "Election Guide," and he produced it in 1885 with a happy readiness for the two great contests that followed. It is a strange and curious thing that with all his gift of utterance Mr. Asquith has since written so little. No other published book stands to his name: and very few articles.* The voice and not the pen is his chosen instrument.

With the increased fullness of his life on every side, Mr. Asquith now moved from John Street to a larger house in Maresfield Gardens, off Fitzjohn's Avenue. He began going into society far more frequently than in earlier days, and he was received everywhere as a rising man, both at the Bar and in Parliament. But with all the calls upon his time and energies Mr. Asquith has always carried about with him a certain atmosphere of ease. He has never been a harassed man. In his most crowded years he had had time

* *E.g.* a preface to an essay on "Liberalism" by Mr. Herbert Samuel; and some reprinted addresses—as, for instance, on "Autobiography" and "Criticism" (1898).

for his fellow human beings. Without being a great talker he takes a great pleasure in society. He was now able to indulge that pleasure more freely.

But this freedom was not to last much longer. In 1892 the Unionist Government had come to the extreme customary limit of Parliament under the Septennial Act. It was necessary for them to bring their activities to a reluctant and drawn-out close. In the General Election that followed, Mr. Gladstone fought a great and splendid combat; but he obtained a majority for Irish Home Rule of only forty votes. " Too small ! " he cried. " Too small ! " Even at this hour of thwarted hopes Mr. Asquith surpassed himself. Far away up in East Fife a furious effort was made by the Unionists to throw Mr. Asquith out of Parliament. They reduced his majority by eighty-two votes ; but that left him a substantial margin to represent East Fife in the Parliament of 1892.

CHAPTER V

HOME SECRETARY

" It is the business of Englishmen to make England worth living in as well as worth dying for. It is both a higher and a harder task to make than to take a City. Patriotism, like charity, begins at home."—MR. ASQUITH.

THE 1886–92 Cabinet of Lord Salisbury was slow to admit defeat. Even after the General Election in the summer of 1892 ministers decided to meet Parliament without resigning office; and when the House of Commons met on August 4, the Conservatives were still sitting to the right of the Speaker's chair. In the debate on the Address, there was an attempt to argue that the country had spoken indecisively, and that the majority was of no account because it was made up of Irish members. Mr. Asquith was chosen by Mr. Gladstone to move an amendment which told the Queen, in the courtly language of such amendments, that the Tories had lost the Election.* The choice was a signal honour and

* " We feel it, however, to be our duty humbly to submit to your Majesty that it is essential that your Majesty's

favour, and Mr. Asquith acquitted himself well. He came to bury Cæsar, and not to praise him. The speech was a great debating achievement. He tore to shreds the arguments for delay, and called upon the House, with the fire of a young Daniel, to " execute the judgment which the nation has pronounced."

It was now clear that the House of Commons had found a new master-voice—one of those few speakers that know how to play on its moods and tempers. Mr. Asquith was already contrasted with Mr. Gladstone—the swift, ruthless march of argument with the rich flow of eloquence—the charmer with the fighter, the " organ-voice " with the sledge-hammer. Here was a new man who was destined to bring into parliamentary debate, after a long period of sonorous and stately rhetoric, a new model of quick, decisive speech.

The amendment to the Address was, of course, carried, and Mr. Gladstone proceeded to form the Ministry over which the old man was to preside for only a year and a few months. There was now no doubt, of course, that Mr. Asquith would receive office. But it was naturally expected that he would have to climb the steep ministerial

Government should possess the confidence of this House and the country, and respectfully to represent to your Majesty that such confidence is not reposed in the present advisers of your Majesty."

stairs by way of an under-secretaryship. He had been in Parliament for only six years; and he had spoken little.

But with a majority of only forty Mr. Gladstone wanted men who were likely to help in tight places; and he and Mr. John Morley * had already marked Asquith as one of such.

Thus it was that when he made up his 1892 Ministry, Mr. Gladstone made Mr. Asquith Home Secretary.

"Sensation" is undoubtedly the word to describe the impression created by this appointment. Perhaps the man least surprised seemed to be Mr. Asquith himself. The young member stepped into the great historic post with perfect composure. He was always very sure of himself.

Such sudden elevations bring lightnings to bear on the head that is raised so high above its fellows, and the House of Commons is a strict and critical court of judgment. Like a social club, the House reserves its own approval as the final stamp of excellence, and no ministerial existence can be safe or sure without it. Mr. Asquith was to find that a great and sudden rise brings with it great and sudden tests. The Government of 1892-5 did not find itself on a bed of roses. Not only was its majority of forty

* Now Lord Morley.

miserably inadequate for its great task, but even that majority was broken up into sections and factions—two Irish parties, an extreme Radical wing, impatient of delay, and a Welsh party, not yet united and harmonised. The Home Secretary shared with his colleagues the distresses of this position. This great secretaryship of State, the most intimate link between the Crown and the people, wields great and wide-spreading power, extending from law to health, and stretching from the factory to the home. The Home Secretary is responsible for the safeguarding of life and limb in the mines and on the railways, in the factories and the workshops. He has powers of life and death; for he can revise all sentences through the privilege of the Crown's mercy now placed in his hands. No office could bring a man into closer contact with the public. None raises more critical points of home policy.

Mr. Asquith made a great Home Secretary. It is the tradition of the Office—and few things are more reliable than these Office traditions—that he made perhaps the best Home Secretary of modern times. He carried zeal and energy into branches of the Home Office atrophied by long neglect. He came after a series of ministers steeped in the tradition of leaving things alone. As long as things are well, no course could be wiser. But things at this time were not well. The great factory-system of the later nineteenth century had far outgrown both law and administration. The fewness of the inspectors made inspection a farce. A great crop of new trades had grown up which were both dangerous in themselves and dangerously conducted. Greed had stifled humanity, and was defying the weak and nerveless hand of the State. Above all, a vast new system of home-work, little differing from slavery, except in the want of responsibility for the worker, had grown up outside the factory system, organised with the deliberate object of escaping all control of any kind.

Mr. Asquith, in 1892-5, took the first steps towards remedying a state of things which is still only half remedied. He organised his inspectors afresh, and added to their number, appointing for the first time women-inspectors to protect and safeguard women-workers ; for he has always been a believer in the extension of woman's work in such spheres. He enforced, through a series of committees, and by means of Orders in Council and Acts of Parliament, a new and far-reaching protection for workers engaged in certain highly dangerous trades—the grinders of Sheffield, the linen-makers of Belfast, the white-lead workers in the Potteries. Only those who know the power of the great industrials in the House of Commons, the fears and timidities of this class of worker, the deadening force of habit and tradition, can realise the patience and perseverance necessary to a Minister who will disturb his peace by the least of such reforms. In high positions the easiest thing of all is to do nothing. It is almost as easy to help the strong. But to use power as a defence for the weak and the helpless—that is always the hardest of all tasks. Throughout these years Mr. Asquith followed that task. He brought all his reforms to a head in the great Factory Act which was finally passed by common consent in 1895, after the fall of the Liberal Government. That Act has since been strengthened and supplemented by an even larger and stricter Labour code.* But at the moment the Act of 1895 marked a great step forward. It definitely widened and broadened the protective power of the State as against those new and formidable dangers to human life, health and liberty which the factory system brings with it.

But although Mr. Asquith showed himself thus the first of the great modern Home Secretaries, he had a more formidable task on other sides of his work. He was the first Home Secretary to

* Not merely in the Consolidated Act of 1901, but in all the new Acts that resulted from the upheaval of 1906—the Sweated Boards Act, the Shop Act, etc.

feel the full vigour of those new forces which have since taken more definite and orderly shape in the Labour Party. At that moment these forces took the form of a vague and querulous unrest, a fierce resentment against a social system which seemed to these new insurgents, hot with the wrath of a new evangel, little better than the hypocritical handmaid of power. This discontent took various forms. There was, for instance, the fierce fight for the right to meet in Trafalgar Square, a claim partly of sentiment and partly of substance, but at that moment a banner of revolt in London, expressing many deeper and fiercer grievances.* Mr. Asquith had the advantage of having mastered this case in his professional duty of defending Mr. John Burns and Mr. Cunninghame Graham for their share in the Trafalgar Square riot of 1887. Perhaps he scarcely even now understood the full meaning of the Londoner's complaint, or the deep resentment—as of Romans excluded from their Forum—that underlay it. But his delay in dealing with it did not last long. He received a deputation in November, 1892, and then issued an order under which, after notification to the police, meetings should be allowed on

* So deeply was this exclusion from Trafalgar Square felt in London between 1887 and 1892, that I knew many respectable persons who became revolutionaries from brooding over it.

Saturdays and Sundays. The extremists were not satisfied. But the edge was taken off the agitation, and this compromise has worked ever since.

He was not to emerge so easily from the next difficulty. In September, 1893, there occurred at Featherstone, in the West Riding of Yorkshire, one of those sudden outbreaks of violence, confused and passionate, which have accompanied the effervescence of the Labour movement at various moments during the last twenty years. Panic seized on the local authorities, and they first applied to the Home Office for more police. Mr. Asquith supplied them. But, as the riot went on, panic became a frenzy of fear, and the same local authorities now sent for soldiery. The soldiers went. They fired into the crowd, killing two men.

Mr. Asquith now had his first experience in public life of bearing the full brunt of a wave of popular fury. He had little difficulty in the House of Commons, where the Labour forces were at that time very weak and divided. It was in the country and on the platform that he was most fiercely assailed. He was pursued by an organised campaign of obloquy and insult. "Murderer!" "Featherstone!" "Who killed the miners?" These were the mildest of the interruptions which broke into his speeches and marred his best periods. There is nothing more harassing to a public speaker. But Mr. Asquith stood his ground like a rock. "Talk about Featherstone!" shouted the Labour men. "I will talk about Featherstone!" answered Asquith, and for the next ten minutes poured in a hot volley of argument on behalf of law and order.

It was not, indeed, until many years had passed—after Commissions had sat and many wise pronouncements been made—that Mr. Asquith allowed the fact to be known that he had not been consulted at all when the troops were sent for to Featherstone—so sudden and hurried was the summons. He thought it his duty to stand by his local authorities; and he placed his public reputation in the utmost peril by doing it. There are few braver acts recorded in public life.

Mr. Asquith showed the same dogged courage in dealing with the case of Mrs. Maybrick, the lady who was convicted of poisoning her husband, and was at that time in prison under a life sentence. Mr. Asquith's old patron, Sir Charles Russell—created Lord Chief Justice in 1894—had convinced himself of Mrs. Maybrick's innocence, and she had many powerful backers. But Mr. Asquith read the evidence, and was unconvinced. He stood up against the agitation, rugged and unperturbed· Justice was in his trust. Not for the greatest in the land would he release a woman whom he considered guilty.

A more serious issue arose over the case of the Irish dynamitards. These were some of those violent and desperate men who, in the early eighties, had organised from America the war of explosives against British life and property. They had been in prison for over ten years, and both the Irish parties were now agitating for their release. Mr. John Redmond pleaded their case in the House with great force and skill; and many British Liberals considered that there was a case for amnesty. It was at this critical parliamentary moment that Mr. Asquith rose and delivered a stern and uncompromising defence of the law. His speech was a stern and final refusal to contemplate the very possibility of any relaxation of the original sentences :—

> " Persons who resort to this mode of warfare against Society, who use dynamite as their instrument, who proceed in their methods with reckless disregard of life and the safety of the weak, the innocent and the helpless, are persons who deserve and will receive no consideration or indulgence from any British Government."

" Mr. Asquith," said Mr. Justin M'Carthy, in the

speech that followed, " has shut the prison door with a clang " The criticism was felt, somehow, to contain some element of the truth. There is nothing in these cases more difficult to define than the proper attitude of a perfect Home Secretary. It lies somewhere between the strict code of the law-courts and the loose humanitarianism of the streets. Mr. Asquith always took a somewhat juridical view of his position, as that of a supreme law-keeper, a sort of super-Chief-Justice. General opinion has decided otherwise. " The quality of mercy is not strained." The Home Secretary in this country appears rather to be the appointed interpreter of forces that lie outside the Statute-book or the law-courts, forces of the largest and broadest kind—political, humane, or even diplomatic. He has to take into account the strife of races and the war of classes. He has to consider the peace of the peoples.

In all such considerations there are, of course, dangers of weakness and sentimentality. As against such tendencies Mr. Asquith stood firmly for the security and solidity of the State. There he performed no mean service.

In 1891 Mr. Asquith had sustained a severe personal loss. His admirable wife, the mother of his five children, had died of typhoid fever while they were on a holiday visit to that beautiful

Scotch island which lies off the Firth of Clyde on the west coast of Scotland—the Isle of Arran. It was a great and bitter loss, and for a time it threw Mr. Asquith's life into great confusion. The boys were sent to Mr. Mansfield's school at Bracknell, and in the holidays he joined them in the country. For the rest of the year he left the house in Maresfield Gardens and lived chiefly in a flat in Mount Street. This homeless existence threw him very much into society, and during 1892-94 he went out a great deal in West London. He joined that interesting and stimulating group of the younger men and women of the time known as the " Souls " ; and it was in this company that he often met and learned to admire Mr. Arthur Balfour. But a more important meeting was that with the young daughter of the great industrial, Sir Charles Tennant. Miss " Margot " Tennant was at that time regarded as the most brilliant and daring young woman in English Society, a great reader, a splendid talker, a youthful friend of the great, a correspondent of Dr. Jowett and Mr. Gladstone. Her fame had already filled the drawing-rooms and her daring defiance of convention formed the theme for those fascinating myths which provide so much of the lighter talk of our great middle class. She was even supposed to have become already the heroine of several novels, and to be able to select, at her will, a husband from among the coming rulers of England.

Mr. Asquith married Miss Tennant in 1894, and Mr. Gladstone went to the wedding. It was a great union, and it restored to Mr. Asquith that domestic life which has always been so large an element in his happiness. The second Mrs. Asquith has always been an excellent friend of her step-children; and thus he has ever since had the advantage of a happy and united home as the background to an arduous life.

Absorbed in his great office, Mr. Asquith took no great part in the larger and higher politics of this Administration. He already saw that the great constitutional struggle which had opened in 1886 was destined to pass on to another phase. In most of his speeches at this time he discussed the question of the House of Lords ; * and it was he who, in one vivid phrase, crystallised the feeling of the Liberal party at that time, face to face with the unbroken opposition of an implacable Upper Chamber. "We are ploughing the sands," he said ; and the phrase summed up the whole three years. It was thrown back on him with mocking laughter by the Tories. But he laughs best who laughs last ; and the phrase gradually

* It is a curious fact that, thinking aloud in these speeches, he rejected the remedy of a limited veto, and suggested the plan of a Referendum.

inspired in the whole party an unshakable resolve not to repeat the experience.

Later on, Mr. Asquith coined another striking phrase. " Yes, the cup is nearly full," he said in 1895, when the life of this Ministry had almost reached its close, " the career of high-handed wrong is nearly come to an end. We have been too long a Peer-ridden nation." It sounds to-day, knowing what we do of subsequent history, like a prophecy of doom.

Looking back on the period of that abortive Government, with its heroic leader spending the last golden sands of his splendid strength in that hopeless onslaught on impregnable privilege, we wonder how those men could have gone on fighting a venture so desperate and forlorn. We marvel at the long patience of those years, the vain expenditure of eloquence and appeal on ears that heard not. Why did not the Liberals of the nineties make that direct attack which was their only way through the entanglement ?

The answer is that this is a country of old and deep-rooted reverences, not easily shaken without prolonged misfeasance and proved recalcitrance. The cup had to be filled. The sands had to be ploughed. The offence of the Peers had to stand out, flagrant and glaring, in the sight of men. Not until that was accomplished would the

British people consent to alter a fabric hallowed by so many memories.

1893-5 was the last effort to move forward along the old lines. It failed ; but looking back on the past, we can see that it was a necessary stage in a great and mighty process of change.

Meanwhile Mr. Asquith himself was to suffer in Parliament from the fixed resolve of the House of Lords to use the powers of veto to the very last cartridge. In 1893, not content with the Home Rule Bill, the Government laid upon Mr. Asquith the task of dealing with the very thorny question of liability for industrial accidents. The old law of employers' liability had been reduced to a dead letter by the lawyers, whose labours, as Blackstone has so shrewdly pointed out, tend to profit most those who pay them best. The judge-made doctrine of common employment had practically relieved the employers of all responsibility. Mr. Asquith straightened out the law and made it clear and simple. If his Bill of 1893 had passed into law, every employer would have been from that time responsible for every accident that was not distinctly traceable to the carelessness of the workman. But at this critical hour all the threatened interests were seeking help from the House of Lords, now immensely strengthened by the refusal of the Liberals to accept

HOME SECRETARY 79

Mr. Gladstone's advice and dissolve over the defeat of Home Rule.* To accept one defeat is to invite a second. A powerful railway company † gained the ear of the Tory Peers, and the Upper House inserted an amendment permitting a general power of contracting out from liability. That dealt a fatal blow; and Mr. Asquith could do nothing else but withdraw the Bill.

It was then, and then only, that Mr. Gladstone was persuaded that the war against the House of Lords must be taken up as the most active aim of the Liberal Party: and he announced that policy in a great speech to the Commons. But the thunder of the cheers had scarcely died down when it was announced that the "Grand Old Man" had retired from the scene.

The confusion that followed is now part of history. The successor to Mr. Gladstone in the Premiership, Lord Rosebery, was selected by Queen Victoria without consultation with Mr. Gladstone himself, who had intended to propose Lord Spencer. Lord Rosebery loyally consulted his colleagues, who approved the choice. But no good could come of such a departure from all the due and deserved precedences of political

* The Home Rule Bill was thrown out in the House of Lords by 419 to 41. The majority in the Commons on Third Reading was 34. The Employers' Liability Bill came to the Lords later.

† The London and North Western.

life. The older leaders sat restlessly under the chairmanship of the young and brilliant Peer; and Sir William Harcourt, the leader of the House of Commons, was at one time scarcely on speaking terms with his own Prime Minister. There was in the new Ministry neither harmony of action nor unity of policy. The country was distracted by a number of rival political cries, and at last the Rosebery Administration drifted helplessly down the stream to the biggest defeat ever sustained by the Liberal party. In the General Election which so unhappily followed a snap defeat on the supply of the new ammunition to the Army in the summer of 1895 the Unionists were returned with a majority of 152.

All through this period of confusion Mr. Asquith went steadily forward with his work, holding himself for the most part aloof from the personal quarrels of the great party chiefs. He was commissioned by the Government to take charge of the Welsh Disestablishment Bill, which was introduced in 1894 rather to satisfy the Welsh party, than with any real hope of carrying it into law. The Bill was a stronger measure than that which ultimately passed into law in 1914, and the Churchmen found Mr. Asquith's attitude hard and unsympathetic. They forgot that he had been brought up in the rugged school of

HOME SECRETARY 81

Yorkshire Nonconformity, and that the traditions and memories of Anglican privilege still worked in his blood. Reading his speeches on the Bill again after this long interval, one is amazed at his mastery of the Welsh case. But it was not through the Anglicans that the shrewdest blow against the Bill was to be delivered. In the Committee stage Mr. Asquith, over-pressed and harassed with domestic cares,* failed to keep in close touch with the Welsh members. Some of them refused their support to the Government on certain crucial details of the Bill, and the majority descended in one division to the figure of two. That settled the fate of the Welsh Church Bill.

Out of the wreck of divided counsels, Mr. Asquith saved one measure—the Factory Bill. This was a Bill very near to his heart. The work at the Home Office had widened and deepened his sympathies with the lot of the labouring poor in these islands. In the speeches of this period we find him speaking of the rising Labour Party with a rare insight and sympathy † all the more remarkable for the fact that he was exposed to their most furious onslaughts. Turning from

* Mrs. Asquith's first child died at birth, and she herself passed through a severe illness.

† January 20, 1893.

G

other confusions, he was preaching Liberalism as a creed for the lifting of the people, a creed " to make England worth living in as well as worth dying for." In an earlier speech we find a passage which splendidly embodies this nobler ambition which every genuine modern statesman since Henri Quatre has kept somewhere hidden away in his heart :—

> "Behind and beneath the surface of Society there are sights terrible, appalling, and yet inspiring for those who have eyes to see. The labourer tills the fields which are not his own season after season with patient industry, with no hope for his old age beyond the precarious bounty of public or private charity. The worker, old before her time, lives a life worse than the mediæval serf in the squalor of the sweater's den. The little child cowers in the cold and the darkness while it listens in terror for thé unsteady step which is to it the signal of its parent's home coming. These surely are figures, if we could only recognise it, more appalling to the imagination and more stirring to the sense of wrong than any vision that ever inspired crusader or knight errant." *

* January 20, 1893.

Perhaps it was because he thus stood fast by the higher faith and held his head well above the confusions of personal faction that in the disastrous conflict of that summer (1895), when so many great leaders were falling, Mr. Asquith came back to Westminster from East Fife with a largely increased majority.* But the Liberal party was scattered and defeated, and Mr. Asquith's first period of Ministerial office had come to an abrupt close.

* From 376 to 716.

CHAPTER VI

OPPOSITION—THE SOUTH AFRICAN WAR

"For friend and foe were shadows in the mist,
And friend slew friend not knowing whom he slew."
                                             TENNYSON.

MR. ASQUITH took a bold step on finding himself out of office in 1895. He went back to the Bar. Prim and pedantic persons found many reasons why this was to be regarded as an outrageous, unprecedented step. It was argued that a Privy Councillor could not plead before the Privy Council; that judges and juries would be fascinated by the nod or intimidated by the frown of an ex-Home Secretary; that rival lawyers would be unduly handicapped in their vital race for business. Mr. Asquith, in fine, had to break through a bad custom; and he did so in his own plain, silent way without any apology or excuse. It was an honest and sensible course. It is now recognised that the starving of ex-Ministers is not so valuable a part of the British Constitution that it requires to be enforced by a compulsory exclusion from the right to work.

When Mr. Asquith donned once more the silk gown of the Courts, he undoubtedly diminished his power of activity in public affairs. After a long day in the Courts, a barrister comes to the House of Commons little inclined to take frequent part in debate. Thus we are not surprised to find that Mr. Asquith spoke less often both in the House and the country during the years following the great defeat of 1895.

Public affairs, indeed, were not for the moment very attractive to Liberal members of Parliament. The immense majority given by the country to the Unionists placed the Government for the moment in a position of unchallengeable ascendancy. This ascendancy had been consolidated by the inclusion of the Liberal-Unionists in the new Government, and Mr. Joseph Chamberlain had brought into the Conservative Cabinet an instinct for popular measures which helped to keep Lord Salisbury and his friends in power. The Workmen's Compensation Act, although it had the defect of all very litigable legislation, carried with it a strong, resounding, assertion of popular right; and Mr. Asquith was too wise to give it direct official opposition. He aimed at extending the scope of its provisions. At the Home Office, Sir Matthew White Ridley, a weak but sympathetic man, carried on, in the main, the traditions of

Mr. Asquith's own administration. Thus it was that although Mr. Asquith performed many of the leading duties of opposition—especially in moving the rejection of Government measures—the main parliamentary fighting of those days passed to a group of able and brilliant free-lances below the gangway, among whom the most conspicuous figures were Mr. McKenna and Mr. Lloyd George.

The real stress and conflict of this period began after 1896 to shift more and more from Home affairs to Foreign and Colonial. The crisis of these years were concerned not with Ireland, which lay almost passive beneath the blow of 1893, but with Armenia, France, and South Africa. It was in regard to these great matters that very gradually there began to appear within the Liberal Party a little rift, at first impalpable, but soon slowly widening until it threatened to silence the music of Liberalism in this country.

It is really difficult to locate the precise watershed at which the two different streams of ideas about the Empire which now began to divide Liberalism really separated. The origins of such divisions are very subtle. It often happens that a chance nickname or phrase may come to stereotype a contrast of opinion which might otherwise be soon merged and forgotten. In this new controversy such terms as " Liberal Imperialist " and "Little Englander" played a great part. But there was often little reality behind those terms. Both schools of thought really believed in the Empire; both believed in this England—

"This precious stone set in the silver sea"—

which is none the less noble for being a little country.

It was rather a question of perspective and proportion—how much the Empire should sacrifice to England, or how much England to the Empire. But it became for the moment one of those deep moral conflicts which cause infinite searchings of heart.

In this division of feeling Mr. Asquith leaned towards the Liberal Imperialists without ever becoming a violent extremist in that direction. Friendship reinforced opinion; for both Lord Rosebery and Sir Alfred (now Lord) Milner, two of the great banner-bearers in this cause, were strong friends of Mr. Asquith. But there was beyond this a profound intellectual belief in the mission of the British Empire as a great civilising influence throughout the world. Mr. Asquith was never tired of saying, in the speeches of this period, that the British Empire was the greatest political invention of man—

"With all its failures and shortcomings, with all its weak places and its black spots, it is the greatest and the most fruitful experiment that the world has yet seen in the corporate union of free and self-governing communities."

No one who has surveyed this wonderful fabric of world-rule, with its high sense of duty in the rulers and freedom in the ruled, can dispute such a judgment. But those who know the conditions of the British masses at home, either in the great " industrial " towns or in the smiling countrysides of England, may sometimes honestly doubt whether the " white man's burden " is not greater than he can bear. It is just round such issues that a sincere difference arose within the Liberal Party, producing a series of crises which threatened to destroy the whole machine.

The first of these crises arose over the massacres of Christian Armenian subjects by the Turkish Government in 1896. The whole of Europe was appalled by these events, which began with massacres in remote regions of Asia Minor far beyond the reach of the British Fleet, but culminated in a gigantic slaughter in the very streets of Constantinople, which was then supposed to be within our easy control.

At this point came the paradox. For it was not the " Imperialists," but the men who were best known for their love of peace and hatred of adventure who now passionately urged that the British Empire should put forth its might on behalf of this bitterly oppressed Christian people.

Lord Salisbury was sympathetic, but doggedly inactive. Mr. Gladstone came out from his retirement and hotly espoused the cause of the Armenians. The great mass of the Liberals, feeling the thrill of the old leadership, began to swing in favour of intervention. It was at this moment that Lord Rosebery announced his resignation of the leadership of the Party, in a speech made at Edinburgh on October 9, 1896.

A letter from Lord Salisbury, since published in the memoirs of Canon Maccoll,* has revealed to the world the fact that Austria, Russia, and Germany had agreed at this moment to combine in support of Turkey in Armenia, in case of our intervention, and that France would probably have come in also on that side. This great Government secret was probably known to Lord Rosebery, and explains his resignation. The pity of it is that he could not safely make it public.

Mr. Asquith probably had some inkling of the

* Pages 153-154, " Malcolm Maccoll: Memoirs and Correspondence." Smith, Elder & Co. 1914.

facts. His speeches on the Armenian question were moderate and restrained, but he kept in touch with both sections of opinion. He was in favour of deposing the Sultan, but pointed out that such a course was impossible if Russia opposed it. He also revealed the fact that in 1894 both France and Russia had refused to join in if force were used; and force was plainly necessary if anything were to be done.

Mr. Asquith was the only Cabinet Minister present on Lord Rosebery's Edinburgh platform on the occasion of the resignation speech. A few phrases dropped by Lord Rosebery gave the impression that he had chosen Mr. Asquith as his successor. But there was nothing to encourage this in the veiled rebuke which Mr. Asquith himself gave to Lord Rosebery on that very platform :—

> "I venture to say to Lord Rosebery in your presence to-night, that leadership is a thing which involves reciprocal claims and reciprocal obligations. It is not in the power of either party to the contract to put an end to it at his own will—and the voice of the other party has not been heard."

Mr. Asquith was quick to perceive the peril involved in the impression that he was to be forced on to the party by Lord Rosebery. Addressing his constituents a few days later, he instantly and emphatically blotted out the impression. In impressive phrases he deprecated all personal quarrels and differences, and suggested patience in the selection of a successor to the leadership. The upshot was that the throne remained vacant for a long period.

But it was destined that the rush of world events should leave no rest to the unhappy Liberal party. At that moment Europe was entering upon a new phase of that prolonged struggle for the unclaimed areas of Africa which is not even yet at an end. France had not yet acquiesced in our occupation of Egypt; and on July 10, 1898, the world was suddenly startled by the arrival at Fashoda, on the Upper Nile, of a brilliant and adventurous French officer, Colonel Marchand. He had traversed Africa from west to east with the consent of the Belgian Government. He now marched his small force of heroic soldiers into Fashoda, claimed it in the name of the French Government, and hoisted the French flag. It has always been the weakness of all who have from time to time occupied Egypt, that

* Lord Kimberley in the Lords and Sir William Harcourt in the Commons acted as Parliamentary Leaders, but no definite leader of the whole party was chosen until 1898.

being dependent on the yearly flooding of the Nile for subsistence and irrigation, that river-land can be choked into submission by any power that gains a grip of that mighty river nearer to its source. This power of control has, of course, been immensely increased by modern engineering.*

The share of France in Colonel Marchand's act was therefore an open challenge to the British occupation of Egypt. For a few days France seemed inclined to support her pioneer; and war seemed inevitable. But a combination of Lord Salisbury's firmness at home and General (now Lord) Kitchener's supple handling on the spot, ended in Colonel Marchand's retreat through Abyssinia. So ended the most serious modern threat to the relations of France and England.

The crisis passed; but it had reverberating effects on the Liberal party. Mr. Asquith had supported the Government throughout, and afterwards claimed that it was only the resulting unanimity that had saved the situation. But there was a section among the Liberal leaders who had long been watching with alarm the growth of Imperialism in the country and Party. Their discontent came to a head in December, 1898,

* *E.g.* the shutting of the gates at the Assouan dam could deprive the whole of Egypt of the water required at certain periods of the year.

when Sir William Harcourt and Mr. John Morley published letters to one another announcing their resignation from the ranks of the Liberal leaders. It looked as if one of the great English parties was about to disappear.

At this critical moment Mr. Asquith kept his head. He had to address the Liberal Federation a few days later. He made a forcible plea for party unity. A few weeks later he made an even more impressive appeal :—

> "Are we, of that party of progress, who for more than one hundred years, through evil and good report, have upheld in policy and in legislation the cause of freedom, and the rights of the common people, in the unending struggle between justice and privilege—are we going to sheath our swords and to lower our flag because upon this point or that of priority or procedure we cannot come to a unanimous agreement? I say no."*

The appeal had its effect; but the very instinct of unity barred off Mr. Asquith himself from the leadership at that moment. It was not forgotten by a section of the party that Mr. Asquith had sat on Lord Rosebery's platform on that fateful evening of Lord Rosebery's resignation. Perhaps,

* February 21, 1899.

too, it was remembered that he had been complimented by Mr. Chamberlain at the famous dinner to Sir Alfred Milner, on his going out to South Africa.* Otherwise, Mr. Asquith, by character, distinction and gift of speech, obviously stood next in order of succession. But he was now known to have a definite leaning towards Imperialism; and the craving of the party, after all these distracting events, was to find a leader who belonged to no section but only to the party.

The choice fell on Sir Henry Campbell-Bannerman. But it was still generally expected that Sir Henry, who was known to have a strong desire for the Speakership, and reputed to have little ambition for leadership, would refuse. Mr. Asquith's friends almost took it for granted that the mantle would fall on him. But to every one's surprise, "C.-B." accepted. Mr. Asquith's time was not yet fully come.

It was the South African war which was destined to bring to a head all these simmering differences. At the outset of the events that led up to that war, Mr. Asquith was the most vigorous opponent of

* March 28, 1897. Mr. Asquith's opponents are glad to recognise in him an honourable, although a formidable, foe. They all rejoiced in the position which he had achieved for himself and which his attainments and character fully deserved."—MR. CHAMBERLAIN on MR. ASQUITH.

Mr. Chamberlain's policy in South Africa. No one condemned more vehemently the crime of the Jameson Raid; no one criticised more searchingly the extraordinary mixture of smooth dispatches and violent speeches which went to make up the Milner-Chamberlain diplomacy. Even after the war had broken out Mr. Asquith continued to condemn the manner in which the British cause had been presented to the world. But on the merits of the case he decided that Great Britain was in the right, and that it was the Boers who were responsible for the war.

That was the view he expressed, speaking only for himself, on the night of the outbreak of the war to a Scotch audience;* and to that view he adhered steadily throughout the following three years. At first he was opposed to the annexation of the Republics; but he ended by acquiescing in the necessity of that step also.

The controversy that rent the Liberal party during the following years threatened the existence of Liberalism in this country. So deep and bitter were the passions aroused on either side— especially over certain incidents of warfare—that it is even now difficult to explain how the party escaped one of those final cleavages which destroy and paralyse great causes. It was an honest

* At Kinnaird, October 9, 1899.

difference of opinion on facts rather than a difference of principle ; and that is perhaps what saved the party. But above all there was the wish to be united. Despite the extremists, there was a small group of men in either section who, looking beyond the passions of the moment, foresaw that, after the war, the Liberal party would still be required as a mighty instrument of peace. On one side " C.-B." and Mr. Lloyd George—and on the other side, Mr. Asquith and Sir Edward Grey—all resisted the splitting of the party. The greatest danger seemed to come when Grey, Asquith, and Haldane followed Lord Rosebery in forming the Liberal League. But even in joining that strange movement they made it clear that final party separation was the very object they intended to avoid.

The Liberal League, indeed, was probably the means of saving the unity of the party. For it provided a temporary refuge for a very great body of opinion which might otherwise have drifted over to the Unionists. It gave the Liberal Imperialists a platform on which to state their ideal of the British Empire as a great instrument of liberty in the world. It was in addressing this audience that Mr. Asquith made speeches which still remain the best expressions of the ideal which the British race, at its best, keeps before it as its sole justification to claim to rule so large a part of the world's surface.

These speeches saved the situation. Listening to them, Liberals of the other school saw that they were not really so far apart. There seemed no real difference of principle beneath even the fierce controversies of the war.

But it was finally agreement on the terms of peace that brought the Liberal sections once more together. The Unionists had no ideas to contribute to the ending of the war. It gradually became clear that "unconditional surrender" meant interminable war. In December, 1901, Lord Rosebery, at Chesterfield, put forward proposals for peace which were practically the same as those which had been advocated by the peace Liberals for the whole of the previous year. Mr. Asquith heartily supported his late Chief, and in 1902 it became the accepted view, agreed to by all parties, that terms had to be made with the Boers. The policy of "drives" had brought the war to its last stage in South Africa; and the Boers had ceased to exist as an army in the field. Finally, the conference called at Vereeniging on March 23 ended in a Treaty signed on May 31. The Boer Republics were annexed to the British Empire; but, on the other hand, self-government was guaranteed. It was by a happy chance that

H

one of the first acts of the Liberal Government, in 1906, was to carry out by Royal Proclamation this solemn promise of Home Rule contained in the Treaty of Vereeniging. In accomplishing that task Sir Henry Campbell-Bannerman and Mr. Asquith worked together. For while " C.-B." was Prime Minister, Mr. Asquith was chairman of the committee which drew up the Constitution for the Transvaal.

The perils to the Empire and the Liberal party came to an end at one and the same time. But among the men who saved both from disaster during these black and critical years, Mr. Asquith played a vital and fruitful part.

CHAPTER VII

OPPOSITION—FREE TRADE

" Instead of raising the price of bread, let us try to raise the standard of life. Temperance, better housing, the tenure and taxation of land, these are matters as to which we have allowed our legislation to fall deplorably in arrear. To take up the task in a spirit of faith and resolute purpose is, I hope and believe, the mission of the Liberal party in a Liberal Parliament."—Mr. Asquith.

In the autumn of 1900 the Unionist Government dissolved Parliament, and asked the country for a vote of confidence to finish the Boer war. The Parliament of 1895 had still two years to run under the Septennial Act; and there are many strong objections, now generally recognised, to a General Election in war time. But at that moment the glamour of Lord Roberts' victories had dazzled the country into the belief that the war was practically over. It was the darkest moment in the fortunes of the Liberal party, now divided and practically leaderless. Mr. Chamberlain was at the height of his power, and he was not the man to let such a chance slip by. For the moment the plan was completely successful. The Unionist Government was returned a second time, on what was known at the time as a "khaki wave," with a majority of 130, only 20 less than in 1895.

This defeat completed the eclipse of Liberalism. There were many Job's Counsellors in that dark hour, and among them were those who attributed the defeat not merely to the war, but to the programme of reforms which had been inscribed on the Liberal banners ever since the famous meeting at Newcastle. Lord Rosebery, always quick to give expression to those passing humours, recommended the party to "clean the slate."

This comprehensive advice from a leader who had himself refused to lead, rather took away the breath of the Liberal rank and file. It is not the way with Englishmen to desert their principles in time of adversity; and Mr. Asquith is certainly not a man built after that model. He made no attempt to follow Lord Rosebery in his general counsels of surrender. He ingeniously tried to explain that this "cleaning of the slate" was simply a "picturesque way" of phrasing his old and shrewd advice to "select and concentrate." A policy of social reform was more than ever necessary for Liberals; for it was quite clear that the Tory Government would do nothing in that direction.* It became obvious from such speeches that Lord Rosebery and Mr. Asquith did not mean the same thing.

The only point on which Mr. Asquith definitely threw in his lot with his brilliant and wayward chieftain was the postponement of Home Rule. There he had been for a long time gravitating in the direction of a policy of postponement until British opinion was more favourable. As far back as 1898 † he had stoutly asserted that as the Irish party claimed to be independent of the British Liberals, the Liberals had a right to be independent of the Irish. While still adhering to the principle of Home Rule, he had declared in that speech that the Liberals should not resume office without an " independent Liberal majority in the House of Commons." ‡

Now, in 1901, he went a step further. On joining the Liberal League he wrote a letter containing the following passage :—

"Is it to be part of the policy, the programme, of our party, that if returned to

* February, 1902.
† December 16, at Birmingham.
‡ Mr. Asquith was often confronted with this opinion in the struggle of 1912–14. But he always maintained that the majority of 1910, was independent of the Irish in the sense that if the Irish were left out altogether the Liberals and Labour party still had a majority.

power it will introduce into the House of Commons a bill for Irish Home Rule? The answer is in my judgment—No."

Not, as he explained, because he had ceased to believe in Home Rule; but because "the end we have in view can only be attained by methods which will carry with them, step by step, the sanction and sympathy of British opinion." This view, he maintained, boldly grasping the nettle, was "not apostasy," but "common-sense." It was, in fact, only the democratic act of bowing to the will of the people expressed in two elections.

It is difficult to say how these counsels would have fared with a party drawn from a class of Englishmen still under the potent glamour of the Gladstone tradition. But at that moment a sudden and startling change took place in the whole atmosphere of domestic politics.

After the close of the war, in 1902, Lord Salisbury resigned from the Premiership in July, and handed the succession to Mr. Balfour. The passing over of Mr. Chamberlain—at that moment ill in bed—was an event of signal importance. With that second victory at the polls the Conservative forces in the country had become more and more impatient of the restraining influence exercised by the Liberal Unionists. The succession of Mr. Balfour gave them their opportunity. They demanded some return for their great sacrifices at the last two General Elections. The parsons, for instance, asked for help in their schools; and the publicans demanded protection from reforming magistrates. They were the artificers of victory. They demanded their wages.

Mr. Balfour surrendered to what was practically his own policy. True, in 1900, he had supported Mr. Chamberlain in assuring the country that the issue was confined to the war. But in politics, as in scripture, text can be quoted against text; and much must be forgiven to the exigencies of electioneering. It is hard to argue with the big battalions; and so Mr. Balfour, after receiving one or two warnings at bye-elections, gave to the parsons the Education Bill of 1902, and to the publicans the Licensing Bill of 1904. The Voluntary schools were to be on the rates; and the liquor licenses were to be freeholds. What more could be desired?

This sudden revival of true blue Conservatism, trumpeted from every pulpit and acclaimed in every public-house parlour, instantly revolutionised the situation within the Liberal party. Mr. Balfour's new policy acted like a magnet on those scattered and divided units. In November,

1902, Mr. Asquith and Sir Henry Campbell-Bannerman appeared on the same platform for the first time after four years. The battle of the programmes was forgotten. The slates were laid aside. The " war to the knife and fork " gave way to the peace of the round table. It was now no longer a question of reforms for the future. It was a bare and stark question of defending that which they had—the treasure-house of freedom achieved. In the midst of quarrelling over the tactics of attack, the Liberals had suddenly discovered that the enemy was plundering their baggage. The process of rally began immediately.

Mr. Asquith has always been above all things a party man. He has always followed Edmund Burke in his splendid and understanding admiration for party. " Party is a body of men united for promoting by their joint endeavours the national interest upon some particular principle on which they are all agreed." * There could be no nobler tie between men in secular matters; and Mr. Asquith has always avowed a robust and healthy attachment to the party tradition. Even in the darkest days of Liberal division he had

* Burke, "Thoughts on the Cause of the Present Discontent."

avowed himself an unregenerate Liberal.* He was never a divider or a separator; he always sought, throughout these controversies, for the common denominator in the widest differences. Therefore it was that he now rejoiced openly in the new reunion and threw himself without stint into the great political campaign which raged from 1903 to 1906.

Once the stream began to flow the pace and volume of its current steadily increased. Everything seemed to work on the side of Liberalism in those crowded years. The Home Rule entanglement was straightened out by an unexpected development of the Schools controversy. In passing his Education Bill, Mr. Balfour found himself obliged more and more to lean upon the support of the Irish Catholic Nationalists, who felt bound to subordinate all other questions to the help and support of these schools which are precariously maintained in England for the children of the forlorn and scattered exiles from

* *E.g.* at Bilston, on December 20, 1901. "I confess to you I am a party man. I was brought up in the Liberal party, and in the Liberal party I intend to remain. Why? Because, in a sentence, the Liberal party, in my opinion, has done more than any other combination that has ever existed to give us freedom and equal laws at home, to secure for us respect abroad, and to create for us loyal and self-governing dependencies."

Ireland. Several times, during the height of that struggle, the Irish members, perhaps at that time soothed by Land Purchase and half hoping for Home Rule from the Unionists, saved Mr. Balfour's Government. They thus clearly notified to the world that there were questions which they regarded as more important than Irish Home Rule. If this were so with Irishmen, it gradually dawned on the most stalwart English Home Rulers that it would be impertinent for them to claim to be more Irish than the Irish themselves. The Asquith policy of postponement took on a different aspect.

Then, in the middle of this new conflict, came a new and startling event—Mr. Chamberlain's attack on Free Trade. Since his great disappointment in 1902, Mr. Chamberlain had been restless and dissatisfied. He disliked the Education Bill, and during its passage through the House he took occasion to undertake his promised journey to Africa. Brooding on the lonely veldt and visiting the graves of the Canadians and Australasians who had died for the Empire, he had been gradually drawn to the conviction that Britain was in their debt and must repay them for their sacrifices. He decided to propose that this repayment should take the form of giving a preference to their goods in the British market.

This was the proposal that Mr. Chamberlain launched on the country on May 15, 1903, entirely on his own authority and in such complete independence of the Cabinet to which he belonged that Mr. Balfour had actually made a strong Free Trade speech immediately before.

It was Mr. Asquith who instantly perceived the tremendous gravity of Mr. Chamberlain's challenge; and as early as May 21, he threw down the gage of an unconditional defiance. In the developments that followed it was Mr. Asquith who, with his power of quick decision and clear speech, soon took a dominating part in the defence of Free Trade. Nor is it a mere biographer's exaggeration to say that in the tremendous conflict of 1903–6 it was Mr. Asquith's speeches that largely turned the scale against Mr. Chamberlain. At first Mr. Chamberlain's campaign undoubtedly made way. Trade was suffering from the depression that always follows wars, and the people were ready for a new evangel. The great Protectionist doctrine would not hold half the world in fee if it had not a specious and attractive side. It is one of those great arguments in which all the short views are on one side, and all the long views on the other; and mankind, as a whole, takes more kindly to short views than to long.

Mr. Asquith saw at once that no time was to be

lost. He followed up Mr. Chamberlain at every step—on the platform and in the House of Commons. Perhaps Mr. Chamberlain himself had scarcely realised at first the implications of his policy. A preference to the Colonies is a perfectly simple and proper thing in a Protectionist country, and has long been the rule in France. But in order to give a preference a country must be first Protectionist; and as the particular imports from the British Colonies include wheat and wool, it is clear that the Protection in such a case would have to extend both to Food and to Raw Materials.

It was along this track that Mr. Chamberlain was driven by the steady and deadly cross-examination of Mr. Asquith. The British people dearly love a fight, whether within the ropes or on the platform; and they watched with an absorbed interest this great strife between Mr. Asquith and Mr. Chamberlain. By the end of May Mr. Chamberlain had been forced to admit in the House of Commons the deadly, damning fact that to fulfil his policy he must tax food. From that moment forward the situation developed rapidly. The tension within the Cabinet became too bitter to last. At last, in September, Mr. Balfour astutely settled the matter by getting rid of both Protectionists and Free Traders, and forming a Ministry of Philosophic Doubt.

Then the fun became fast and furious. All through that autumn Mr. Asquith hunted Mr. Chamberlain through the country. It was a fight between a whale and a sword-fish. Mr. Chamberlain, with his immense power of demagogic appeal, his skill in invective, his daring habit of open public bribery, always seemed at first to be making a great impression. But then came Mr. Asquith with the still, small voice of pertinent inquiry, with the embarrassing habit of accuracy in facts and figures, with the crushing advantage of a mind trained and skilled in economic controversy. "No one denies my facts," cried Mr. Chamberlain. "All they do is to quarrel over my figures." To which Mr. Asquith, with crushing finality—"If your figures are wrong, how can your facts stand?"

These speeches now stand as a monument of public dialectic, skilful, trenchant, and victorious.* When the process was over, Mr. Chamberlain's case was smashed and pulverised. The "raging, tearing propaganda" which he had gaily welcomed was turned against itself. The case for British Free Trade stood "foursquare to all the winds," stronger for the storm through which

* "Trade and the Empire. Mr. Chamberlain's Proposals." Methuen & Co. (6d.)

it had passed, proved and tried by tempest and hurricane.

In his speech to the Unionist Free Traders on May 17, 1904, Mr. Asquith summed up the issue of the controversy :—

> "It was quite true that one or two things were wanting—simple things, commonplace things; a little logic, a little arithmetic, and a little history; but if the doctrine failed, as he believed up to the present it had, it was because it had to encounter and overcome one of the most formidable and insurmountable ramparts of the whole wide world—the common-sense of British people."

He might have added that this same British common-sense had the good chance to find a voice in the speeches of Mr. Asquith.

CHAPTER VIII

CHANCELLOR AND PRIME MINISTER. 1906-10.

"One fire drives out one fire; one nail, one nail;
Rights by rights falter, strength by strength do fail."
Coriolanus.

IN December, 1905, Mr. Balfour at last resigned office, and Sir Henry Campbell-Bannerman immediately proceeded to form a Government.

Mr. Asquith's services to the party during the last three years in the fight for Free Trade had raised his claims very high. It was obvious to every one that his position was second only to that of the Prime Minister. Sir Edward Grey was the inevitable Foreign Secretary. There was only one other post equal to Mr. Asquith's record—and that was a post regarded in modern times as very high up in the Cabinet, the Chancellorship of the Exchequer. When this was offered to him, Mr. Asquith took the post without any of those qualms which characterised the acceptance of the office by other members of the Liberal Imperialist group. Thus, after more than ten years of opposition, Mr. Asquith once more returned to Whitehall as a leading member of a Liberal Cabinet.

The General Election which followed in January resulted in a majority for the Reform parties without parallel in modern times. Including the Nationalists, the Progressive parties in the new House of Commons had a majority of 354 over the Unionists. Without the Nationalists, the Liberals and Labour members had a majority of 271 over the Unionists. Even if the Nationalists had coalesced with the Unionists the Liberal and Labour men would still have had a majority of 108. It seemed as if for once the cause of progress had swept away all impediments. The new Cabinet appeared invincible in its strength. No one who played any part in that time will forget the overwhelming sensation of achievement and expectation which inspired the new Parliament of 1906. It seemed as if, after a long period of stagnation, the British people were about to enter upon a path of bold and rapid reform.

Within a year all these hopes were dashed to the ground. The unthinkable thing had happened. The House of Lords had within a year of its election deliberately defied the power of this new House of Commons. To do this, the Peers chose an issue which had played almost a leading part in the recent election—the Education question. For the question of the control of the public rate-supported Elementary Schools raised by the Act of 1902 was second only to Free Trade in the election campaign of 1905-6. A moderate and reasonable compromise, little liked by the Radical extremists, and approved by even the Catholic Irish, was contemptuously destroyed by the House of Lords at the bidding of the English Bishops.

Faced with this rebuff, the House of Commons once more, now as in 1893, shirked a direct conflict with the House of Lords. It is true that a series of strong resolutions in favour of limiting the Lords' Veto were carried through the House of Commons in the spring of 1907. But no action followed. Once more—from 1907 to 1909—a Liberal Parliament proceeded to " plough the sands." The House of Lords had flourished too long on a diet of threats to regard mere Resolutions with any fear. Hard words, even when embodied in resolutions, break no bones. So now the Lords proceeded to do just as they pleased with the legislative projects of this great Progressive House of Commons. In 1907 they rejected the Scotch Land Bills. In 1908 they defied even the Bishops by throwing out the English Licensing Bill, a great reform sorely needed—as events have since proved—to meet the most pressing of national evils, and supported by the moderate men of all parties. But the gravest defiance of the popular Chamber was reached in 1909, when the Lords threw out the famous Budget framed by Mr. Lloyd George to meet the great new financial needs arising from the increase of the Navy and the grant of Old Age Pensions.

Such were the events in the life of this first great Liberal Ministry—grave and pregnant events, gradually leading up to the most tremendous Constitutional struggle through which Great Britain has passed since the Civil Wars of the seventeenth century.

Mr. Asquith was Chancellor of the Exchequer for two years and a few months—from 1906 to the spring of 1908. The Lords in those days made no claim to control finance : and thus for the moment Mr. Asquith held in the Ministry perhaps the most powerful position next to the Premiership.

But he was not tempted by that position to any daring new departures in finance. He devoted his energies steadily to the great task of redeeming the Exchequer from the confusions into which it had been thrown by the South African war. That war had added £100,000,000 to the National Debt.

Before Mr. Asquith had left the Exchequer he had practically wiped off the whole of that sum, and restored the debt to the position it held before the Boer War.*

Mr. Asquith had frankly admitted to the country that he could not reduce both debt and taxation at the same time. But he managed to wipe off some of the war taxation. In the course of his Chancellorship he abolished the export duty on coal, took a penny off tea, and a farthing off sugar.

The last and greatest act of Mr. Asquith's Chancellorship was to introduce a wide and comprehensive scheme of Old Age Pensions. But in April, † 1908, before he had faced the task of making financial provision for this scheme, Sir Henry Campbell-Bannerman, sick and worn out by many labours, resigned from the Premiership.

Mr. Asquith was chosen by King Edward VII. as "C.-B.'s" successor, with the full approval of the whole Liberal party. He travelled to Biarritz, where the King was spending the last few months

---

* In 1889 the National Debt stood at £697,000,000. In 1903 it stood at £770,000,000. Mr. Austen Chamberlain wiped off nearly £30,000,000, so that in 1906 it stood at £743,000,000. In 1909 it stood once more at £696,000,000, or practically the same as in 1889.

† April 5.

of his life, and there kissed hands as Prime Minister.

In the reorganisation of the Ministry that followed, the principal change was that Mr. Lloyd George succeeded Mr. Asquith as Chancellor of the Exchequer. Mr. Lloyd George found himself instantly faced with a tremendous financial crisis, due not merely to the increase of the Navy, but to the fact that the House of Commons had immensely enlarged and extended the grant of pensions to the aged poor.* It became necessary to throw the new taxes either on the rich or the poor. Mr. Lloyd George decided to do neither exclusively, but to tax each in proportion to their ability to pay. He even dared to levy a few very small taxes on the ownership of land. Both in the Cabinet and in the House of Commons Mr. Asquith was throughout that great and famous struggle the most loyal and determined supporter of Mr. Lloyd George's proposals.

When the Lords threw out the Budget, Mr. Asquith took up the challenge with all the vigour of his nature. There was something in this act of the Lords which roused all his profoundest

---

* The annual sum for Old Age Pensions estimated in Mr. Asquith's Budget in 1908 was £6,000,000. The actual sum required has since turned out to be £13,000,000. By taxes on tobacco and drink Mr. Lloyd George threw a large part of this burden on to the class that profited by it.

instinct for constitutional order and practice. He stood firmly and without any compromise by the rights of Commons.

All through this year of the great Budget struggle (1909), with its stormy vicissitudes of loss and gain, with its hopes and fears, its light and its darkness, Mr. Asquith steadily hoped for peace. He found it almost impossible to believe that the Lords would throw out the Budget. This belief in a peaceful issue was shared by his Cabinet, men long accustomed to ordered ways, and slow to believe in earthquakes. But there were great forces driving the Lords forward. There were the landowners, hating the land-taxes; the brewers, loathing the license-duties; the Tariff Reformers, seeing their own scheme of taxation beaten out of the field; and all that various and motley crowd of offended interests that gathers against a reforming Government in its later years.

In the summer of 1909 it was understood that both Lord Lansdowne and Mr. Balfour refused to sanction the idea of rejection. But in the autumn the Anti-Budget Barons had organised themselves, and threatened to defy the leaders. The Tariff Reformers had recovered from the shock of the onset and were making way in the country. The first giddy popularity of the Budget seemed to be waning. The engineers of the voting-machine undertook to defeat it in the country. So, after long hesitation, the murder was perpetrated. The Budget was thrown out.

Into the fight thus opened Mr. Asquith threw himself with all his powers of indignation and energy. "In matters of finance," he said at Birmingham, on September 17, "the Lords are impotent, and the Commons are supreme." From that view he never deviated by a single hair's-breadth right through this great controversy. In all his speeches on this action of the Lords there is a passion of luminous conviction—a kind of glowing white light. It was the light of insight into the governing principles of the British constitution.

On December 2, Mr. Asquith moved in the House of Commons a solemn resolution denouncing the action of the House of Lords as "A breach of the constitution and usurpation of the rights of the Commons." He announced a Dissolution; and such was the feeling at the moment that the House of Commons received its death warrant with a tempest of cheers.

The country was now up against realities. For owing to the action of the Lords the Commons could not even collect taxes, and therefore they could not govern. There was only one course left in this issue: that was for the people to decide between the two Chambers.

It was the breach of the spirit of the constitution which filled Mr. Asquith with so genuine an anger.

Faced with this anger, Mr. Austen Chamberlain had remarked at Birmingham that " the pedantry of lawyers " left him cold. This exposed him to Mr. Asquith's fiercest rebuke :—

> " It was pedantry of this kind—the pedantry which realises and dwells upon the distinction between the genius and the spirit of our Constitution on the one side, and the bare and barren letter of the law upon the other—it was pedantry of this kind which made and saved the liberties of England. It was pedants, like Pym and Selden and Somers, who rescued this House largely through the power of the purse from the domination of the Crown. We need not be ashamed to be called by the same name and to bear the same reproach if, acting in the same spirit and using largely the same weapons, we put an end to the usurpations of the House of Lords."

In this passage Mr. Asquith revealed his true political pedigree. Pym, Selden, and Somers—

there is the sequence to which he belongs as a Parliamentary leader. It is a noble sequence. For it is these men that have saved England from being a land of chronic revolutions, and given to this "land of such dear souls, this dear, dear land," the golden quality of a refuge and a haven for threatened liberties.

The General Election was fixed for January, 1910, and there was no time to be lost. On December 10, in the Albert Hall, Mr. Asquith announced positively that the absolute Veto of the Lords must cease. At the same time he released himself from his pledge to hold back over Irish Home Rule. The Veto was to go, and the Lords were to pass after three years all measures on which the British people were continuously resolved. One of the measures to be submitted to this test was Irish Home Rule.

The General Election that followed resulted in the return of 275 Liberals, 273 Unionists, 40 Labour men, and 82 Irish. This gave Mr. Asquith a majority of 124 at the best; but as ten of the Irish were independent, and several of the Labour members were doubtful, he emerged with a working majority of little more than 100, composed almost entirely of Irish and Labour men.

Both sides were disappointed. The Tariff Reformers had hoped for a crushing Unionist majority. Eager Liberals had expected a repetition of 1906. But no Government can rule without losing votes, and the Liberals had been ruling for four years. The revival of Home Rule and the fear of the Budget had thrown the Free Trade Unionists back into the Conservative ranks. The rich men had taken fright, and " the curse of the poor is their poverty."

On the whole the result was not so bad. But there was a great fall from excessive hopes. For a moment Mr. Asquith's Government hesitated as to their next step. There was a talk of placing Lords' Reform in front of Anti-Veto. But Mr. John Redmond spoke firmly at Dublin; and the Liberal rank and file in Great Britain stood firm. Finding that the army was undismayed, the leaders soon rallied from the shock. They perceived that their followers were willing to follow them into the breach. The quantity was diminished; but the quality was better than ever, tried as by fire. So they moved forward on that arduous and perilous task of asserting the liberties of England against the power of privilege and riches in the richest country of the world.

The spring of 1910 was occupied in passing through the House of Commons the resolutions on which was to be based the Bill limiting the

Lords' Veto. These resolutions fell into two parts. The first abolished formally and for ever the power of the Lords over finance. The second applied to ordinary Bills. It was a scheme propounded nearly half a century before by Mr. John Bright, limiting the Lords' Veto over Bills to three rejections in three sessions. Here was still a cumbrous and tedious delay for the process of reform, but better than the closed door.

The resolutions were resisted line by line and word by word. But Mr. Asquith pressed them steadily through Parliament, conceding nothing of substance to the powerful and highly organised opposition. Scarcely was this process accomplished when King Edward VII. died. The event came as a shock to the country, and it seemed unfair to the new King that his reign should open in conflict. King George V. suggested peace, and for a moment there passed over the parties one of those remorseful waves of feeling which come in the midst of civil strife. A conference of party leaders was arranged—four from each side,*—and these great authorities held private sessions all through that summer while the rank and file murmured and fretted outside the closed doors.

* Liberals: Mr. Asquith, Mr. Lloyd George, Mr. Birrell, Lord Crewe. Unionists: Mr. Arthur Balfour, Lord Lansdowne, Mr. Austen Chamberlain, and Lord Cawdor.

The proceedings of that Conference have never been revealed. It is certain that there was at one time a prospect of agreement on certain broad lines of national settlement between those who met at the round table. But the bold terms of peace that might have ended civil strife did not commend themselves to the hotter partisans without. It was quite clear that the parties were not willing to follow their leaders in proposals that would practically have abolished the old dividing lines between the British parties. There are times when grave civil differences can only be decided, if at all in a peaceful way, by the prevailing power of a majority.

After twenty meetings the Conference came to an end without a decision. On November 10, Mr. Asquith made this result known to the House of Commons, and at the same time announced a second Dissolution. He had already made it clear that on the issue of this election the whole result of the struggle between Commons and Lords depended. It was, in fact, a sort of King's Election. For it had long been understood, even in the days of Edward VII., that the Monarchy would require a special General Election on the issue before consenting to use, on a sufficiently large scale, the Royal prerogative of Peer creation. And it was now clear that without the use of that Prerogative the resistance of the Lords could not be overcome.

The General Election took place in December, 1910, and the result was almost precisely the same as that of the previous election in January of the same year.*

Thus the year 1911 opened with Mr. Asquith still in power, and possessing from the country a full and complete mandate to overpower the resistance of the House of Lords.

* There was a net Government gain of two seats, giving a full majority of 126, or a working majority of about 100.

CHAPTER IX

CIVIL STRIFE AND FOREIGN WAR

" But soon a wonder came to light,
   That showed the rogues they lied;
The man recovered from the bite,
   The dog it was that died."
                            GOLDSMITH'S " Elegy."

THE great struggle between Lords and Commons had now reached a new phase. The two General Elections of 1910 had given the Asquith Government a decisive victory in the country. It remained for them to reap the fruits of victory in Parliament itself.

There is nothing finer in Mr. Asquith's parliamentary career than his navigation of this cause through the House of Commons during the Session of 1911. He had to face stormy seas. The Unionists had been beaten in the country, but they were still very strong at Westminster. They refused to accept the verdict of the country as valid on any issue. They obstructed; they defied; they clamoured. There was an evening in this struggle when, for the first time in his life, Mr. Asquith was refused a hearing by the Commons. Mr. Asquith worked his ship steadily forward through this hurricane without departing an inch from his fixed course. He conceded nothing of substance. He carried the Parliament Bill through the House of Commons as a strong, effective assertion of popular rights, a worthy successor in the great line of constitutional measures that have moulded and developed the governance of these islands, from Magna Charta to the Act of Settlement.

But meanwhile, as the Bill drew nearer to the Upper House, there were constant movements of drawing-room plotters and country-house conspirators—" Die-Hards," " Backwoodsmen," and other desperate characters. Some of the Peers, recalling their Norman ancestry, talked openly of physical force. When their leaders wavered, they met, they grouped, they organised, they cajoled, they threatened. The country, it was already clear from the by-elections, was thinking of other things —sick-insurance, labour-exchanges, land-reform. That was the very reason why it was considered necessary, by the strategists of this movement, that the House of Lords should die a startling death—consumed, like Sardanapalus, in the blaze of its own self-lit funeral pyre.

CIVIL STRIFE AND FOREIGN WAR 127

The Parliament Bill reached the House of Lords in July. The Peers gave it a second reading, and then proceeded to riddle it from end to end with amendments. For Veto-limitation they substituted Reform and Referendum. They abolished the Royal Prerogative. They sent the Bill back, in short, as a measure for strengthening the power of the Lords and weakening the power of the Commons.

There was nothing new in all this. It was only "pretty Fanny's way." It was precisely the fashion in which the Lords had treated all Liberal measures for the past twenty years. Mutilation had become a matter of habit.

But on this occasion they were to meet with a surprise. Mr. Asquith very firmly rejected all the Lords' amendments, and sent back the Bill precisely in its original form. There was a great rally of the Peers to defeat it, and the "Backwoodsmen" were ready to face any consequences. Then the bolt fell. Very calmly, but very definitely, Lord Morley informed the Peers that the King had consented to the use of his Prerogative for the full passage on the Bill into law. In other words, the writs were ready for summoning some five hundred Peers to Westminster, pledged to pass the Parliament Act.

Death by adulteration is an ignoble end for a

proud nobility; but that was the Gorgon's head which now faced the British Peers. Their line of battle faltered and wavered. It broke into groups. There was a hubbub of conflicting counsels. Now, as in 1832, a body of "Trimmers" appeared between the parties and decided the issue. At the very last moment in the final division, a body of some forty Peers passed across the House from the left of the Woolsack to the right, and saved the purity of the British aristocracy. The Bill became an Act by a majority of seventeen votes. " 'Tis enough—'twill serve."

From start to finish, in this bold assault upon privilege armed and defiant, Mr. Asquith had never wavered from the logical results of his policy. The lists of the new Peers had been made out. Some four hundred British * families trembled on the brink of ennoblement. Every detail had been observed, even to the very plans for seating this new and enlarged Second Chamber in the solemn and stately precincts of Westminster Hall.

Mr. Asquith's victory was now complete: the Unionists could find no other consolation than righteous and vocal indignation. On August 7, they moved a Vote of Censure in the House of

* It had been arranged, in 1911, as in 1832, that the Peerages should be given largely to collaterals of existing Peerages or to several members of the same family.

Commons on the Government for their use of the Prerogative of the Crown. "A felon blow," cried Mr. Balfour. Thus attacked, Mr. Asquith seized the opportunity for giving to the House a full and frank statement of the whole series of transactions between Crown and Cabinet during the previous six months. He revealed the understanding under which the General Election had been conducted, an understanding necessarily kept secret out of consideration for the Crown itself. He protested that if he had consented to a second General Election without some security for its effectiveness he would have been false to his post. He ended on a lofty note :—

> "My conscience tells me that I have consistently striven to uphold the dignity and just privileges of the Crown. But I hold my office not only by favour of the Crown, but by the confidence of the people ; and I should be guilty indeed of treason if in this supreme moment of a great struggle I were to betray their trust."

There had been no more convincing and silencing defence made in the House of Commons since Sir Robert Peel, in that last stately and moving Third Reading speech on the Corn Law Repeal Bill, justified his action in freeing the food of the people.

The storm centre now shifted to Irish Home Rule. For Mr. Asquith had clearly stated, ever since the beginning of 1910, that he intended to use the Parliament Act to pass Home Rule. His tactics of postponement had ended with the final victory of Free Trade. He proposed to pass now into law a measure in which he had always profoundly believed ever since his first election to Parliament on this very Home Rule issue in 1886. The Opposition leaders and organisers had made full use of the anti-Home Rule feeling in 1910. By including Home Rule in his election programme, Mr. Asquith had then undoubtedly lost the vote of the Unionist Free Traders, and probably a considerable body of that moderate, timid English opinion which had supported the Liberals in 1906. It would have been absurd and flagitious if having paid this penalty in England and given this pledge to Ireland Mr. Asquith had now hesitated.

He did not hesitate. The Home Rule Bill was introduced early in 1911 and passed through the House of Commons, after a prolonged parliamentary struggle, in the course of 1911 and the January of 1912. It was the measure of 1893 considerably improved and straightened out in its drafting, and with a simple and satisfactory

CIVIL STRIFE AND FOREIGN WAR 131

solution of several of the problems which had most vexed Mr. Gladstone.*

From the very outset of this new Home Rule struggle the Unionist Opposition had but one demand and one only—a new Dissolution. They had denied that the last General Election gave a mandate for the Parliament Act. They now denied that it gave a mandate for Home Rule. It was quite clear, even to the humblest Liberal, that on these lines dissolutions might go on for ever—or until the result went against them. Mr. Asquith, therefore, had the whole party at his back in meeting this demand for a new Dissolution with a dogged and defiant " No ! "

Foiled in this approach, the Unionists now entered upon a desperate venture. As the months passed on, it became clear that Mr. Asquith's majority in the House—only once defeated in Committee on a financial point—would avail for the passage of Home Rule. The Bill passed its first stage under the Parliament Act on January 16, 1912, by a majority of 110 on the Third Reading ; and its passage into law over the heads of the recalcitrant Peers was now only a question of two years' patience. Faced with this situation,

* *E.g.* the question of the Irish Members at Westminster. Mr. Gladstone halted between inclusion and exclusion. Mr. Asquith split the difference and cut the representation down to forty.

the Unionists took the grave resolve to enter upon a design for the defeat of Home Rule by methods outside the Constitution.

As the passage of Home Rule grew nearer, the Ulster Orangemen had taken steps more and more menacing in the direction of preparations for rebellion. With great pomp, a solemn League and Covenant of resistance was prepared and signed in November, 1911, at Belfast. Drilling began throughout Ulster, at first in secret, and then openly. Arms began to be imported under the very eyes of the authorities.

In all these steps Sir Edward Carson, one of the foremost Unionist leaders, was taking a leading part. Mr. Balfour had resigned the leadership of the Unionists in October, 1911, and Mr. Bonar Law had taken his place as leader in the Commons. Mr. Balfour had coquetted with the Ulster movement, but he had never gone further than expressions of sympathy. On June 12, 1913, however, Sir Edward Carson was able to announce at Belfast that Mr. Bonar Law would lead the whole of the Unionist Party into line with the Ulstermen in whatever steps they might take, whether within or without the law. It was the first time since 1745 that a great English party had definitely associated itself with a threat of rebellion.

CIVIL STRIFE AND FOREIGN WAR 133

Mr. Asquith was now faced with a very serious menace to the peace of the realm. He had to choose between coercion and conciliation. There was a strong case for coercion. The Crimes Act stood to hand, a weapon forged originally by the rebels themselves. The Arms Act could be re-enacted. The Common Law alone was probably enough. There was a party in the Cabinet strong for coercion.

Mr. Asquith preferred conciliation. He had a deep belief in the healing effects of time. " Wait and see "—a phrase casually thrown out in the House—had become with him almost a policy. His immense tolerance inclined him to take risks for peace. A convinced party man himself, he could allow much for the extravagances of party feeling. Like the veteran in Browning's poem, he had seen many leaders of revolt. He believed much in eleventh hour repentances.

Above all, he did not want to baptise Home Rule in the blood of Irishmen, or to counter-sign it with their captivity. That desire played a very strong part with the Irish Nationalists, who, during 1912 and 1913, earnestly implored the Government not to employ coercion.

But as the months of 1913 and 1914 wore on, the situation grew darker and darker. Lord Loreburn, in September, 1913, ingeminated peace;

and in October Mr. Asquith made a public offer of overtures, which was publicly accepted by Mr. Bonar Law. But these overtures came to nothing. Neither party meant the same thing or pursued the same object. There could be no real Home Rule without ending the Ascendancy of Ulster; and Ulster would not relinquish that Ascendancy without a struggle. The Orange party grew bolder and bolder. Drilling took place now quite openly, and correspondents went over to write it up. Arms were imported more and more flagrantly. The Unionists looked on uneasily, many of them deeply disturbed in mind. But Mr. Bonar Law's pledge bound them; and however little they may have meant by their earlier threats, now "their faith unfaithful kept them falsely true." They, the party of law and order, now realised that they were drifting rapidly towards the Niagara of civil revolution.

So, gradually and almost imperceptibly, while the politicians were prattling of insurance and Marconi shares, the country moved towards the tremendous crisis of the summer of 1914. In the spring of this year, the Home Rule Bill was approaching its final stages under the Parliament Act. The air was full of rumours of violence. Mr. Asquith was still striving after peace. On March 8, he offered to allow the Ulster counties

CIVIL STRIFE AND FOREIGN WAR 135

to "contract out" of Home Rule for six years by a bare majority vote. Sir Edward Carson refused the offer with scorn. "We do not want a sentence of death with a stay of execution for six years." A few days after, at Bradford, Mr. Churchill spoke of going forward and putting "these grave matters to the proof"—a gloomy and ominous phrase. There were movements of the Navy and Army towards Ulster; accusations of "plots" and counterplots; daring importations of arms by adventurous raiders; timid attempts of the Government to protect their own officials. Much as in 1912, but now far more passionate and electric.

Then suddenly, like a crack of thunder from a heavy, lowering cloud, came (on March 20) the crash. A hundred officers at the Curragh had resigned. A hundred more at Aldershot threatened resignation. The Army was divided: the Fleet was uncertain. The country was face to face with an abyss of civil strife.

At that extreme moment of crisis (on March 30) Mr. Asquith took a step which is perhaps the greatest act of State in his whole career. He made himself Secretary of State for War as well as Prime Minister. This simple act of taking charge—an act taken entirely on his own initiative and without consultation with the Cabinet—

brought a sudden calm and hush to the storm. It cut the Gordian knot of the " Gough memorandum," and the Seely resignation, and all the barbed entanglements of those weeks. The officers went back to their posts. There was a lull.

The Home Rule Bill passed its final third reading in the Commons on May 25. On June 23 the Government introduced into the Lords an Amending Bill to carry out Mr. Asquith's offer to Ulster. The Lords, now confident of recovering their lost power, turned this peace measure inside out and made it a positive injury to Ireland. The deadlock seemed tighter than ever. It was at this moment—on July 21—that Mr. Asquith, faced with a new crisis of which only now we can realise the full and dreadful meaning, accepted a last proposal for peace made from the Throne itself. The King summoned to Buckingham Palace representatives of all the parties concerned, including Sir Edward Carson, Mr. John Redmond, and Mr. Dillon. In the King's summons, he made use of remarkable and significant words—" The cry of civil war is on the lips of the most responsible and sober-minded of my people." It was understood that his address to the delegates included a reference to foreign affairs so grave and significant that it was not included in the published report.

CIVIL STRIFE AND FOREIGN WAR 137

But the warning of the King was of no avail. On July 24 the Conference broke up without coming to any agreement " in principle or detail." On July 26, there was an arms-raid in Dublin Bay, a conflict between the mob and the soldiery, and several lives were lost. On the following day (July 27) a stormy debate on these incidents came as a strange accompaniment to the grave statement of Sir Edward Grey about the European crisis—the clash and rattle of faction still rising high above the sombre undertone of growing world strife.

On the following day (July 30) Mr. Asquith announced the postponement of the Amending Bill, owing to the gravity of the European situation.

* * *

Then the lights of Europe went out, and the squabble over Tyrone and Monaghan to which, at that moment, the Home Rule quarrel had narrowed itself, gave place to a fight for the command of the world. So there we leave that drama of civil dissension—suddenly broken off in mid-action—never, let us hope, to be taken up again in the same spirit.

* *

In face of the world crisis Mr. Asquith became in a moment another man. Before the possibility of civil strife, he had shown at every stage a shuddering reluctance to advance along the road of force—a reluctance that should claim the respect of all men who are able to realise the full meaning of the thing called civil war.

But now he was brought to a real test of faith and conviction. Should we honour our bond? Should we be true to our plighted word to Belgium —aye, and to France? That was the simple form in which the matter presented itself to Mr. Asquith from the very first beginning of the conversations between the Governments that led up to the great strife.

Ever since the Agadir crisis Mr. Asquith had closely followed the daily course of foreign affairs. Like the other members of that inner Cabinet which in these days control the secret courses of foreign policy, he had emerged from the Agadir crisis of 1911 deeply impressed with the menace of Germany's power. Certain phrases and actions of the German Emperor at that time had perhaps more deeply impressed these men than all the known and published despatches or movements. We know now, from Mr. Winston Churchill, what grave steps Mr. Asquith had taken for the strengthening of the Fleet and how seriously he viewed the future.

Then had come the Balkan wars and all the events that followed. All through those months

CIVIL STRIFE AND FOREIGN WAR 139

of 1912-13 Germany had worked hand in hand with Great Britain. The whole atmosphere had changed. Suspicion had given place to trust; mutual fear to confidence. The British Government had undoubtedly fallen off their guard. Thus the war and the diplomacy that led up to the war came on them with a sudden and tremendous shock of surprise.

For a few days the Cabinet were puzzled and divided. Two members resigned. Others went into the war with some doubt.

Not so Mr. Asquith. From the moment that the die was cast, he moved forward unhesitatingly. It was, I think, not so much on this or that point that he judged Germany—not on a clause in a Treaty or a move in the diplomatic game—but on a broad insight into the character and tendency of the Potsdam policy, leading up to the verdict, not so much reasoned as instinctive, of a straight, honest, humane mind.

But with Mr. Asquith, as well as the rest of the Cabinet, it was the invasion of Belgium that settled the matter. On Saturday, July 31, the Cabinet still stood doubtful. On Sunday, August 1, the first steps were taken towards the invasion of Belgium. On Monday, August 2, after one last desperate effort to save Belgium by diplomacy, Great Britain resolved on war. By the story of those three days the whole intervention of Great Britain is illuminated and explained; and with it the spirit in which Mr. Asquith entered into this great affair.

This is the spirit that fills all those great speeches, still fresh in the public memory, with which Mr. Asquith opened the war: the "infamous proposal" speech of August 4; the speech of September 4 at the Guildhall, and the subsequent speeches in the country. The first great House of Commons speech—the speech in which he announced war—was made with little preparation. It was almost an impromptu utterance. Mr. Asquith's heart was full of a tremendous indignation, and the words came into his mouth. Taken all together, these speeches will probably take their place by the side of the oratory of Chatham and Pitt, as among the finest war speeches in the English language.*

His own utter conviction of the righteousness of the war was expressed in one flashing sentence at the Mansion House:

"For my part, I say that sooner than be a silent witness of this tragic triumph of force over law and of brutality over freedom, I

* Guildhall (September 14), Edinburgh (September 18), Dublin (September 25), Cardiff (October 2). Published by the Liberal Publication Department. 1d.

CIVIL STRIFE AND FOREIGN WAR 141

would see this country of ours blotted out of the pages of history."

It is with that high conviction and resolve that Mr. Asquith entered into the war ; and it is in that lofty spirit that he now presides over a national Government, coalesced from all parties, with the sole aim of achieving victory.

CHAPTER X

CHARACTERISTICS

" The first quality of a Prime Minister in a free country is to have more common sense than any man."—
Horace Walpole.

In the hall of Sidney Sussex College, Cambridge, there hangs the famous portrait, with " warts and all," of Oliver Cromwell, painted by that versatile Dutchman * who was equally deft in the counterfeit presentment of Roundhead or Cavalier. No one who looks carefully at this wonderful picture of rugged, resolute strength can fail to be struck by its likeness to Mr. Asquith.

There are differences. " Old Noll's " mouth is cast in a sterner mould : his eye has looked on blood. But the outlines are the same. Both belong to the same breed—to the breed of resolute Ironside men whom Englishmen love to follow.

It is not a breed that excels in the outer graces.

* Sir Peter Lely, born near Utrecht, in England from 1641-1680, and painter for King Charles I., Cromwell, and King Charles II.

CHARACTERISTICS 143

Such men often lack the charm of the lighter social manner. They rarely achieve the Pauline mastery of being "all things to all men." They think more of principles than of persons. That is perhaps why they appeal so to those vast dumb masses who ask for bread rather than smiles.

Prince Rupert, a great soldier with all his faults, once said that the presence of Cromwell in the field was worth an army. As with Cromwell on the field of battle, so with Mr. Asquith in Parliament. His presence is worth a party. His coming changes the face of debate. When he is sitting on the Treasury Bench, Parliament is conscious of its master.

Let me take one scene from an unpublished notebook of recent events :—

> "It was half-past three o'clock in the House of Commons on Monday, July 12, 1915. Mr. Asquith had just slipped into the House from behind the Speaker's chair to answer those questions to the Prime Minister which are always placed at a convenient point on the Order Paper. It was a critical afternoon in the war. Not abroad or at the Front in Flanders, whence Mr. Asquith himself had come hot-foot from counsel with the French Ministers, still ruddy with the breezes of the

English Channel. Not abroad—but at home, where the voices of faction were already heard muttering at the doors of Downing Street.

" There was a curious stillness in the House. For weeks past a little body of sharpshooters had been 'sniping' the Government from below the gangway, and now they had taken advantage of an unhappy political incident to concentrate their fire on the Treasury Bench.

" The Prime Minister's question-sheet was crowded with just that kind of question that free-lances pour in on a Government when it is considered to be showing signs of distress.

" The House was very still. Just as a football crowd watches a critical shot at a goal, men were watching to see whether the Government or their tormentors would come off best in this duel.

" As Mr. Asquith came in there arose an encouraging cheer from all sides of the House. It was a significant indication of the direction in which the sympathy of the House was drifting. It showed the current.

" Mr. Asquith cheerily sat down. There was no smile on that granite-cut face, but there was a shining radiance of confidence which seemed to put a new spirit into the troubled House. He sat down next to Mr. Bonar Law, and looked round the House. He took up his order-paper, nodded, squared his shoulders, and gave that curious little shift back into his seat which always means that he is in a resolute mood.

" The first tormentor rose and put his question. The others were to rise one by one—there were to be supplementaries—cheers and counter-cheers—at least half an hour of fine spirited campaigning.

" Mr. Asquith rose and looked at his order-paper.

" ' I will answer questions 53, 54, 55, 56, and 57 at the same time,' he said; and then, turning, he delivered a terrific rebuke, his voice vibrating with stern passion.

" It was enough. He had asserted his authority. The rebellion was over."

There you have Mr. Asquith in his very element. Parliament is to him as the water to the fish. It has been said of him that he could speak to the House of Commons in his sleep. But, after all, his greatest power is not speech, but his gift of brevity or even of silence. He has the supreme Olympian faculty of being able to rule the Commons by a nod or a shake of the head.

It is this easy masterfulness which gives to Mr. Asquith his real power over Englishmen—that strong nation that always loves a strong ruler.

Yet Mr. Asquith has his softer and milder side. Even in public life he can be gay enough when he likes. "I see in to-day's *Times* that the twin rockets have let each other off," he said to a public meeting on the occasion of the famous joint resignation of Harcourt and Morley. In private his wit is always kindly and often boyish in its merriment. "They don't often catch you napping," he said to the greatest of his Chief Whips when he found him dead asleep from fatigue. He loves to sport with his children, and he is as a rule, with those near him, a thoroughly genial and hearty companion. To his intimates, indeed, he is rather the comrade than the Chief; to his family the fond and best-beloved of fathers; to his secretaries, the most loyal and tolerant of masters; to his Cabinets the best of friends—quick to praise, slow to blame, large, generous, appreciative, helpful.

Yet always there is this feeling of power behind—the feeling that here you have one who, if the need should come, is ready "to smite once, and smite no more."

There is the secret of his mastery.

* * * *

Like all healthy, strong Englishmen, Mr. Asquith loves recreation. He reads many novels—chiefly novels of the old-fashioned type, for he is little in love with modernism and realism in fiction. He plays auction bridge. He is still as fond of the theatre as when he was a boy. Rather late in life he took to golf, and although he does not aspire to be a mock-professional he plays a good steady game. Although starved of sports in early life, he still loves them with a true British devotion.

How, then, explain his reputation for being a remote, rather austere figure—

"—in Logic a great critic,
Profoundly skilled in Analytic"

—icily distant, frigidly detached from the warm daily life of humanity?

The explanation lies partly in his habit of aloofness. He goes rarely into the Lobbies and smoke-rooms of the House, and then passes rapidly, seeing few. "Mr. Gladstone is going blind—he did not see me to-day." It is the old complaint of the "average man." Humanity is hungry for recognition. The great party leaders often meet this desire half-way. "How is the old complaint?" was "Dizzy's" way of gratifying the hunger; and however old the complaint, the heart became young again. Mr. Asquith cares nothing for such arts. He loathes the more vulgar aspects of party management and organisation. It requires all the scourging of the Whips to bring him to the point of popularising himself. He is almost a Coriolanus in this matter of reserve. Being shy himself he flatters others by believing that they, too, object to those raidings of the soul which men call familiarity. So he flies from the Treasury Bench to his private room. On his holidays he goes off with his family to some remote spot in Scotland. He has, as far as I know, never been interviewed; he cultivates no Press following. To Fleet Street he is the least accessible Prime Minister that ever lived only a mile away in Downing Street.

Still, with all this, Mr. Asquith is a friendly, family, very human man; and it is perhaps precisely because he reserves his best for his own circle that he shines so in that smaller sphere. Speaking to the Newspaper Society in 1902,* on behalf of his fellow public men he himself put, with admirable good humour, his own side of the case:—

"We are for the most part a quiet well-meaning set of men, with modest ambitions,

* May 7.

neither better nor worse, I suppose, than the majority of our fellow-creatures, but ordained by the chances of life to pass a considerable part of our life in public. What is the result? We are good for 'copy': you report us, or you misreport us—quite unintentionally, of course—or, still worse, you abstain from reporting us."

There is the true note of the man—an entire absence of vanity, a business-like desire to have his political utterances properly and duly recorded, but otherwise a confirmed wish to be left alone to live his life in his own way. The House of Commons had recently a curious touch of this when this cold and self-contained leader broke out into a sudden flame of passion at the mere shadow of a suggestion that he should accept dictation in the expenditure of his private income.

It sometimes happens that some great talker will be invited to Downing Street to converse with Mr. Asquith. The great talker will perhaps be at the top of his form, talking, like the fallen angels,

"Of Providence, Foreknowledge, Will, and Fate," *

when Mr. Asquith will be found to have silently

* "Paradise Lost," Book II.

slipped away to join in the boisterous talk of the younger members of the party. For although so often regarded as stiff and hard, he really loves to unbend. Perhaps those great talkers would themselves unbend sometimes if they were Prime Ministers.

For it is only the habit of wearing motley at times that can save either in health or reason any man who bears on his shoulders such burdens—"Atlantean, immense"—as the Prime Minister of the British Empire in the twentieth century. The health record of recent public men—"C.-B." and Mr. Chamberlain, for instance—has shown the effects of the strain placed on the delicate human machine by these increasing loads of care and responsibility. Each day of a Prime Minister, taken by itself, is, from dewy morn to sombre eve, one long succession of worries and cares. To bear such a life for long—or even for the appointed years of a Ministry—a man must have many gifts. Mr. Asquith starts with the gift of amazing health. He told a meeting some years ago * that he had not spent two consecutive days in bed for twenty-five years, nor drunk half a dozen bottles of medicine in his life. But the secret of his splendid health is probably to be found in the wholesome and sensible capacity for throwing off care.

* June, 1901.

Mr. Asquith has in a supreme degree that *mens aequa in arduis*—that habit of keeping a steady mind in difficult places—which the wise Roman poet told us to preserve. It is that very steadiness of mind that makes him cling to his rest-days. If Mr. Asquith did not spend his week-ends away from London, and snatch every off-day for golf, he would be crushed by the mountainous burden which fate has thrown upon him.

Thus, being thrown into perpetual daily contention, he loves peace when he can ensue it; prefers games to the mimic strife of argument; and regards talk rather as a by-play than as a serious pursuit. He loves to listen to Lord Morley: but not even that greatest of modern talkers can often draw him into earnest contention about the abstract. For Mr. Asquith, to be accurate, is not a man of the philosophic type. He cares little for large, vague speculations. He is essentially a man of affairs—and of to-day's affairs. Talk is to him a form of business; and when business is over he prefers to read or amuse himself.

Some observers, deceived by this lighter aspect of Mr. Asquith, have suspected him of a want of serious, sustained energy. There they are quite wrong, as Mr. Walter Long, now his fellow-worker, and always a great gentleman, has

recently testified with characteristic generosity.*
If, indeed, Mr. Asquith had been a man of such a temper, he would scarcely a few months ago have added the labours of the War Office to the cares of the Premiership.

But it is easy to see now these observers have been deceived. For Mr. Asquith is an amazingly quick worker; and, like all quick workers, he crowds into a few hours the decisions which occupy the days of other men. "Place the facts before him," said a colleague, who had worked with him for long, "and the decisions come as from an automatic machine." He rarely hesitates or worries about a decision. He gives it promptly and finally, and so keeps well abreast of his work. But such workers can rarely work long hours. They "sweat the sixty minutes to the death"; and on the heels of such labours come great fatigues.

Mr. Asquith's habit during Session, is to start his work at eleven o'clock in the morning and to work all the day at Downing Street and at the House, until dinner-time. He dislikes after-dinner work, and discourages all-night sittings

* "Throughout this long, trying and anxious period the Prime Minister has taken neither holiday nor rest. He has been at his post continuously, day in and day out."—(July 15, 1915, Westminster Hall.)

of the House—which are, truly, perhaps the absurdest of our British institutions. He clears off the work of the day on the day. He prepares his own speeches. His business interviews are short and sharp; and he wastes little time in vague talk. He sees many people in his private room at the House of Commons.

In dealing with his Ministers he does not attempt a close and daily supervision of the work of his Cabinet. The scope of a modern Cabinet of twenty is too vast. But he encourages them to come to him in any difficulty, and probably three or four will see him every day. He is indulgent to their individual schemes and proposals, and rarely crushes them unheard. He prefers that new ideas should come before the Cabinet. For he is a profound believer in Cabinet rule. He would far rather rule as Chief of a ruling Cabinet than as sole autocrat of these isles.

Hence, as Chief of Cabinet he always rides with a loose rein. It is his plan to encourage initiative both in administration and in legislation. Therefore he is slow to intervene until trouble has really arisen. Then he intervenes decisively. No Chief of Cabinet can be firmer at a crisis.

But in ordinary times he works this difficult system of common responsibility with a saving sense of humour. He jests with the House of

Commons over the extravagances and indiscretions of his younger colleagues. "Boys will be boys," seems to be his unspoken comment. He refuses to set up a false idol of Cabinet infallibility—a form of worship that has brought down many Cabinets with its own grotesque weight. He often saves a situation by a simple, human, friendly jest, as if the House of Commons were one great family. There, as in so many other things, the secret of his power is that he is a great "House of Commons man."

It needs be that quarrels must come in Cabinet life; and when they do come, Mr. Asquith is the most fatherly and persuasive of peace-makers. But all such jars cause him great pain. He has an almost excessive sensitiveness about personal matters. He has the English dislike for "scenes." This dread of emotion sometimes causes misunderstandings. When something very painful has to be done, he prefers to do it by letter. Few people find that pleasant. When the Coalition Government was formed, for instance, Mr. Asquith dismissed those old colleagues who had to be dropped for want of room by the singularly frigid method of a circular type-written letter. These unlucky ones were a little hurt, especially as it was their stars and not themselves who were at fault. They were not in the least soothed by the fact that in the House of Commons Mr. Asquith spoke of his parting from them in a voice that broke with emotion. And yet it was the simple fact that he dismissed them by letter solely in order to escape the pain of so many personal partings.

Every one who has served under Mr. Asquith in his Cabinet agrees that he is a wonderful Chairman of that strange secret Committee, the only Committee in this country that keeps no record of its proceedings. The Cabinet has no rules and no standing orders; and so it depends for its peace on the day to day control of its Chairman, the Prime Minister. Mr. Gladstone introduced the custom of divisions into one of his Cabinets—that of 1880-4. The results were deplorable, and perhaps led up to the split of 1886; for the tendency was to produce parties in the Cabinet as well as the House. Mr. Asquith allows no divisions. He sums up the general sense of the Cabinet, splits the difference, compromises, persuades, smooths, postpones, and generally keeps the machine efficient and well-oiled. The Seely affair gave the impression that he was too free and easy in his management of his Cabinets. But a modern Cabinet cannot be controlled like the Cabinets of the eighteenth century. The Coalition Cabinet will probably give him some shrewd tests.

But it has already worked easily for several months; and probably no other man than Mr. Asquith could work it at all.

One result of this genial go-easy way of treating his Cabinet may be seen in the extraordinary power of personal loyalty that Mr. Asquith can command from those who work under him. In a Premiership now moving on towards the decade (1908–15) Mr. Asquith has had no serious personal difference with any colleague. He and Mr. Lloyd George, strongly contrasted in many aspects of character, have worked together through all these years without a single hitch; and the loyalty of Mr. Lloyd George, now as ever, is only equalled—it cannot be surpassed—by the loyalty of Sir Edward Grey. The difficult task of sacrificing Lord Haldane on the altar of a Coalition necessary for national safety, was only rendered possible by this element of personal trust and confidence. Even when colleagues like Lord Morley and Mr. Burns differ in principle, they still retain the same strong sense of personal loyalty to their old Chief.

In tactics, Mr. Asquith is essentially and on principle a "one day" man. Like a steeple-chaser, he moves from point to point. He takes each fence as he comes to it. He does not, in the popular phrase, "make trouble." "I've had a lot of trouble in my life," said the old man on his death-bed, "and most of it never happened." Mr. Asquith will never be able to say that. "Wait and see" expresses an ingrained habit of hopefulness; a refusal to aggravate the worries of the day by thinking of the morrow; a belief that difficulties have a tendency to straighten themselves out, that the magic of cure is always at work in human affairs. No man has ever been more true to principle, or to the long views and deep faiths that arise from principle. "Opportunism," therefore, is not a fair taunt. But in finding the means to a given end—as, for instance, in working his way to the consummation of Home Rule—Mr. Asquith is always amazingly flexible and adaptable. He will horrify the strict partisan by his open-mindedness. He will frighten the faithful by his readiness to bargain and parley.

It is his way: and it succeeds. Watch him in Parliament. Just when his critics are prophesying a fall, he is well over the fence and riding towards the next. Each new difficulty threatens destruction; but he still survives. By his very success he achieves new strength, until his invincibility becomes a legend and a power. The reason is— he believes in himself. He belongs to those of whom it was said, *possunt quia posse videntur*— "they can because they think they can." He has now a great record of parliamentary success behind him; and with each new success he builds up the credit of confidence.

This easy handling of the rudder makes good going for those statesmen who, as in Great Britain, have to depend on public opinion to fill their sails. In such a case " luffing " is not " trimming." It is the art of the skilful helmsman who knows that if he loses the wind he cannot sail his ship at all.

But with Mr. Asquith this day to day flexibility is combined with a grim tenacity on vital matters. Take his attitude on the German quarrel. He keeps a free hand as to details of settlement. But since November last he has never varied a single line or word from the broad objects which he has set before the Allies. Perhaps it is for that very reason—because his faith and aims are so well and deeply founded—that he has never, in the darkest hour, declined from his sunny, hopeful outlook. Standing on the bridge, and looking forward into the thick fog of war, he bids us be of good cheer.

There we must now leave him, First Minister of Great Britain at the stormiest hour of her fate, Pilot of Europe in the hurricane; a man of many cares, but also a man of iron duty and stalwart faith, and therefore serene and unafraid.

MR. ASQUITH'S LIFE

Principal Dates

Born at Morley, in Yorkshire	September 12, 1852
Educated at City of London School	1862-1869
Elected as Scholar of Balliol	1869
University career at Oxford	1870-1875
Called to the Bar	1876
Marries Miss Helen Melland	1877
Enters Parliament as M.P. for East Fife	1886
Defends Mr. Cunninghame Graham and Mr. John Burns	1887
Junior to Sir Charles Russell in Parnell Trial	1889
Becomes Q.C.	1890
First Mrs. Asquith dies	1891
Returned again for East Fife	1892
Becomes Home Secretary	1892
Featherstone Riots	August, 1893
Introduces Employers' Liability Bill	1893
Marries Miss Margaret Tennant	1893
Introduces First Welsh Disestablishment Bill	1895
Passes Factory Act	1895
Leaves Office with Liberal defeat in Commons	July, 1895
Is elected third time for East Fife	1895
Returns to Bar	1895-1905
Joins Liberal League	February, 1902
Leader of Free Trade defence	1903-1905
Chancellor of Exchequer in Liberal Cabinet	December, 1905

160 HERBERT HENRY ASQUITH

Becomes Prime Minister on death of Sir Henry Campbell-Bannerman .. .. April, 1908
Wins his first General Election as Prime Minister January, 1910
Constitutional Conference May to September, 1910
Conference breaks down .. October, 1910
Wins his second General Election as Prime Minister .. December, 1910
Passes Parliament Act 1911
Passes Home Rule Bill for first time 1912
Passes Home Rule Bill for second time 1913
Passes Home Rule Bill for third time .. 1914
Army Crisis .. .. March, 1914
Becomes Secretary of State for War as well as Prime Minister .. .. .. March 30, 1914
Outbreak of Great War: Lord Kitchener becomes Secretary of State for War August, 1914
Forms Coalition Government as Prime Minster 1915

BOOKS USED OR QUOTED

"Life of Mr. Asquith," by J. P. Alderson. With five illustrations. 284 pp. 8vo. Methuen and Co. London, 1905.

"The Right Hon. H. H. Asquith, M.P. A Biography and Appreciation," by Frank Elias. 248 pp. 8vo. James Clarke and Co. London, 1909.

"An Election Guide. Rules for the Conduct of Elections," by H. H. Asquith, Barrister at Law. National Press Agency. 1885. 8vo.

"Liberalism," by Mr. Herbert Samuel. With an Introduction by Mr. Asquith (5 pp.), On Principles of Liberalism. Grant Richards. 1902.

Speeches by the Right Hon. H. H. Asquith, M.P., from his first appointment as a Minister of the Crown in 1892, to his accession to the office of Prime Minister in April, 1908, selected and reprinted from the *Times*. 335 pp. 8vo. The *Times* Office. London, 1908.

"Trade and the Empire," Mr. Chamberlain's proposals examined (being Mr. Asquith's Free Trade speeches). Methuen and Co. 1903. 8vo.

"Ancient Universities and the Modern World. Address by Mr. Asquith." Glasgow. 1907. 8vo.

"Fallacies of Protection" (translation of Bastiat's "Economic Sophisms," by Mr. Patrick Stirling). With an Introductory Note by Mr. Asquith. 1909. 8vo.

"The Premier's Call to Arms." Speech delivered at the Royal Albert Hall before the first 1910 Election, December 10, 1909. Edward Lloyd. London. (Reprinted from the *Daily Chronicle*.)

"Home Rule from the Treasury Bench." Speeches during the First and Second Reading debates of 1912. With an Introduction by Mr. Asquith. 1912. 8vo.

"The Pocket Asquith," compiled by E. E. Morton. London, 1914. 8vo.

The Liberal Publication Department have published authorised versions of practically all the important speeches of Mr. Asquith, and they can be obtained, generally for one penny each, from 41, Parliament Street, W. The Eighty Club have published the speeches made by Mr. Asquith to that body.

The best authority for the Parliamentary speeches is, of course, the Report of the Parliamentary Debates, generally known as "Hansard," but now under official control.

For speeches outside Parliament I have used the reports of the *Times*.

INDEX

ABBOTT, Dr. Edwin, mentioned, 9; his impressions of Mr. Asquith, 9, 11
Agadir crisis, 138
Albert Hall, 1909, speech at, 120
"Angel in the House, The," quoted, 41
Anti-Gambling League Case, 43
Armenian massacres, 88, 89
Arnold, Matthew, quoted, 18
Asquith, Joseph Dixon, mentioned, 3, 4
Assouan dam, 92

"BACKWOODSMEN, the," mentioned, 126
Bagley Wood, 22
Baines, Sir Edward, mentioned, 6
Balfour, Arthur, mentioned, 75, 117, 122, 129, 132; becomes Premier, 102; resigns, 111
Balkan wars, 139
Balliol College Scholarship won, 16; fellowship, 32
Bar, career at the, 35, 40, 42, 45, 61, 84
Barrett, Professor Sir William, mentioned, 7
Bartlett, Sir Ellis Ashmead, 28
Belfast, drilling at, 132, 134, 136

Belgium, invasion of, 139
Bickley, life at, 6, 9
Birmingham, speech at (1909), 118
Birrell, Mr., mentioned, 122
Bishops and Bills in the House of Lords, 113
Boer War, the, 94–97, 99, 114
Bowen, Lord, mentioned, 61
Bright, John, mentioned, 52, 122
Browning, mentioned, 133
Buckingham Palace, Home Rule Conference, 136
Budget, Lloyd George's, thrown out by House of Lords, 114
Burke, Edmund, Mr. Asquith and, 104
Burns, John, defence of, 44, 70; mentioned, 156

CABINET ruler, Mr. Asquith as 153–156
Campbell-Bannerman, Sir Henry, appointed Premier, 94; and Treaty of Vereeniging, 98; on the same platform as Mr. Asquith, 104; resigns, 115
Canonbury, residence in, 6
Carson, Sir Edward, 132, 136; quoted, 135
Carter, Bonham, mentioned, 42
Cawdor, Lord, 122

INDEX

Chamberlain, Austen, quoted, 119; mentioned, 122
Chamberlain, Joseph, mentioned, 37, 85, 94, 95, 99, 102, 103, 150; his greeting of Mr. Asquith's maiden speech, 54; attack on Free Trade, 106–110
Chancellor of Exchequer, Mr. Asquith as, 111, 114, 115
Characteristics, 142–158
Children, Mr. Asquith's, 32, 42, 75
Churchill, Lord Randolph, mentioned, 50
Churchill, Winston, quoted, 135, 138
City of London School, education at, 6, 7, 9
Collins, Churton, mentioned, 24
Commons, House of, Mr. Asquith enters, 48; maiden speech in, 52; and House of Lords, 112, 113, 116–129
Coriolanus," quoted, 111
Corn Law Repeal Bill, mentioned, 129
Crewe, Lord, mentioned, 122
Crimes Bill, Mr. Asquith's maiden speech on the, 52
Cromwell, Oliver, likeness to, 142
Crossley, Sir Francis, mentioned, 4
Crown, the, use of the Prerogative of, 127–129
Cumner Hills, mentioned, 22
Curragh, resignation of officers at the, 135
Curzon, Lord, mentioned, 19

" DIE HARDS, the," mentioned, 126
Dillon, Mr., 136
Dublin, arms raid in, 137

Economist, the, mentioned, 42

Education Bill of 1902, 103, 105
Egyptian questions, 91, 92
Eighty Club, the, mentioned, 52, 55
" Election Guide," Mr. Asquith's, 62
Employers' Liability Bill, 78, 79

FACTORY Bill, 69, 81
Farnley Wood plot, mentioned, 2
Farren, Nellie, the actress, mentioned, 15
Fashoda difficulty, the, 91
Featherstone Riots, 71, 72
Fife (East), Mr. Asquith first returned as M.P. for, 45–47; strenuous Unionist efforts to defeat Mr. Asquith at, 63; increased majority at, 83
Firth, Sir Thomas Freeman, mentioned, 7
Free Trade, the great attack upon, 106–110
Fulneck School, 5

GELL, Lyttleton, mentioned, 29
General Election of 1886, 45; of 1892, 64; of 1895, 80; of 1906, 112; of 1910, 120, 124
George, Lloyd, mentioned, 86, 96, 116, 122, 156; appointed Chancellor of Exchequer, 116
Germany's power, reference to, 138
Gillroyd Mill Company, mentioned, 3
Gladstone, Mr., mentioned, 3, 8, 14, 52, 59, 60, 63, 65, 76, 89, 131, 147, 155; defeat of his first Home Rule Bill, 46; Eighty Club dinner to,

INDEX

55; and war against the House of Lords, 79; his retirement from House of Commons, 79
Godstow Bridge, mentioned, 22
Goldsmith, Oliver, quoted, 125
Graham, Cunninghame, defence of, 44, 70
"Gray's Elegy," quoted, 125
Grey, Sir Edward, mentioned, 19, 96, 137, 156

HALDANE, Lord, mentioned, 62, 96, 156
Hampstead, life at, 41, 62
Hansard, quotation from, 53
Harcourt, Sir William, mentioned, 80, 91, 93
Henri Quatre, 82
Home Rule Bill, the first, 46, 48; rejected by House of Lords, 79; new bill, 130–137
Home Secretary, Mr. Asquith as, 64
House of Commons, Mr. Asquith enters, 48; maiden speech in, 52; and House of Lords, 112, 113, 116–129
House of Lords, the, appeals before, 61, 62; Mr. Asquith and question of, 76, 78, 79; struggle between the House of Commons and, 112, 113, 116–129
Huddersfield, residence in, 5, 6
Hyndman, mentioned, 29

IRISH dynamitards, 73
Irish Home Rule, frequency of speeches on, 56, 58; majority for, 63; 1911 Bill, 130–137
Irish representation at Westminster, 59
Irving, Henry, 15

JAMES, Lord, of Hereford, 61
Jameson Raid, the, mentioned, 95
Jowett, Dr., mentioned, 17, 32; his sermons and influence, 18–20
"Julius Cæsar," quoted, 34

KEATS, quoted, 41
Kimberley, Lord, mentioned, 91
King Edward VII., death of, referred to, 122
Kinnear, Boyd, M.P., defeated by Mr. Asquith, 46
Kitchener, Lord, mentioned, 92

LABOUR Party, Mr. Asquith and, 81
Lansdowne, Lord, mentioned, 19, 117, 122
Law, Bonar, appointed Leader of Unionists, 132; his acceptance of Home Rule overtures, 134
Liberal Federation, address to, 93
Liberal-Imperialists, 86, 96
Liberal League, the, 96, 101
Licensing Bill of 1904, 103
Lincoln's Inn, Mr. Asquith enters, 35
"Little Englander," the term, 87
London and North Western Railway Employers' Liability Bill, 79
London, school days and early life in, 6, 7; sights of London, their influence on Mr. Asquith's early life, 10
Long, Walter, mentioned, 151
Lords, the House of, appeals before, 61, 62; question of, 76, 78, 79; struggle between Commons and, 112, 113, 116–129

Loreburn, Lord, mentioned, 19, 133
Lowe, Robert, 8
Lyttelton, Alfred, mentioned, 52

M'Carthy, Justin, quoted, 73, 74
Maccoll, Canon, memoirs of, referred to, 89
McKenna, Mr., mentioned, 86
Maiden speech in the House of Commons, Mr. Asquith's, 52
Marchand, Colonel, and Fashoda, 91, 92
Marconi shares, mentioned, 134
Marriage, Mr. Asquith's first, 40; his second, 76
Maybrick, Mrs., case of, 72
Milner, Lord, mentioned, 19, 24, 31, 87, 94, 95
Morley, Lord, mentioned, 56, 93, 127, 151, 156
Mowbray, Sir Robert, mentioned, 24

National Debt, and South African War, 114,
National Liberal Federation, 56
Newcastle programme, the, mentioned, 100
Newspaper Society, speech to the, 148

"Ode to the Nightingale," quoted, 41
Old Age Pensions, 114–116
Orangemen, Ulster, and drilling, 132, 134, 136
Oratory, Mr. Asquith's early practice at, 9
Oxford, Bishop of, mentioned, 24
Oxford, life at, 17–33
Oxford Union Society debates, 25; resolutions in, 29

"Paradise Lost," quoted, 149
Parliament, Mr. Asquith enters, 48
Parliament Bill and House of Lords, 127
Parnell, mentioned, 48, 57, 60; Parnell Commission, 57, 60
"Parnellism and Crime," 44
Patmore, Coventry, referred to, 41
"Pedantry of lawyers," the, Mr. Asquith's reply, 119
Peel, Sir Robert, mentioned, 129
Peers, creation of, 123, 127, 128
Phrase-maker, Mr. Asquith as a, 76, 77
Pigott Case, the, 44, 45
Pimlico, life in lodgings at, 7, 12
"Ploughing the sands," 76
Portsmouth, Lord, Mr. Asquith tutor to, 35
Premier, Mr. Asquith chosen, 115
Privy Council, appeals before, 61, 62, 84
"Protection," proposals for, 106–110

Queen Victoria, her selection of Lord Rosebery as Premier, 79

Raleigh, Thomas, mentioned, 24
Redmond, John, mentioned, 136; and Irish Dynamitards, 73; speech at Dublin, 121
Ridley, Sir Matthew White, mentioned, 85
Roberts, Lord, 99
Rosebery, Lord, as Premier, 79; his administration defeated, 80; resignation o

INDEX

leadership, 89, 90, 93 ; and Liberal League, 96
Russell, Sir Charles (afterwards Lord), Mr. Asquith as junior to, 44

SALISBURY, Lord, mentioned, 42, 49, 64, 85, 89, 92 ; resigns Premiership, 102
Salt, Sir Titus, mentioned, 4
Sartor Resartus," quoted, 17
Saturday Review, the, mentioned, 42
Scotch Land Bill, rejected by Lords, 113
Souls, The," 75
South African War, 94–97, 99, 114
Spectator, the, mentioned, 42
Speeches, early, 9, 12 ; maiden speech in House of Commons, 52
Spencer, Lord, 79

TENNANT, Miss " Margot," and the " Souls," first meeting, 75
Tennyson, quoted, 84
Theatres, Mr. Asquith's early liking for, 15
Times, the, mentioned, 57, 58, 146 ; and " Parnellism and Crime " case, 44
Toole, John, the actor, mentioned, 15
Trafalgar Square and public meetings, 44, 70
Turkish Government and Armenian massacres, 88, 89
Tyndall, Professor, mentioned, 7

ULSTER Orangemen, drilling at Belfast, 132, 134, 136
University career, Chap. II., 17–23 ; scholarships won 16, 31
University Extension Movement, 36–39

VEREENIGING, Treaty of, 97, 98

" WAIT and see," 133, 157
Walpole, Horace, quoted, 142
War, Secretary of State for, Mr. Asquith as, 135
War speeches, Mr. Asquith's, reference to, 140
Warren, Sir Herbert, mentioned, 21 ; quoted, 30
Welsh Disestablishment Bill of 1894, 80–82
Willans, John, of Canonbury, life with, 6
Willans, William, of Huddersfield, mentioned, 4
Willans, William Henry, life with, 7, 12
Wimbledon, University Extension Movement lectures at, 37
Women Factory Inspectors, first appointed by Mr. Asquith, 68
Workers in dangerous trades, legislation for, 68, 69
Workmen's Compensation Act, 85
Wright, Mr. Justice, quoted, 43 ; mentioned, 61

YORKSHIRE, Mr. Asquith's pride in, 2, 3

THE END

PRINTED BY
WILLIAM CLOWES AND SONS, LIMITED,
LONDON AND BECCLES.

AN UNDYING STORY OF
UNPARALLELED HEROISM

READ

Ashmead-Bartlett's

THRILLING
DESPATCHES
FROM THE

DARDANELLES

With Large Scale Map

1/- net.

The Standard: "Steering skilfully amid the difficulties presented by the censorship Mr. Ashmead-Bartlett has told in a graphic and lucid manner the full story of the sanguinary fighting in the Gallipoli Peninsula."

The Graphic: "Brilliant accounts of the wonderful operations against Turkey. Vivid, tense, full of matter and facts, these despatches deserve to be preserved by any one who wishes to keep an intelligent eye on the war."

Of all Booksellers, or post free 1/2 direct from

GEORGE NEWNES, Ltd., 8-11 Southampton Street, Strand, W.C.

Authentic Biographies of

LEADING STATESMEN

Crown 8vo, cloth, Portrait Frontispiece

2/6 net per volume

DAVID LLOYD GEORGE: By H. du Parcq.

> An interesting and intimate record of the life of the Minister of Munitions.

WINSTON CHURCHILL: By A. McCallum Scott, M.P.

> A concise and complete life by a well-equipped writer.

SIR EDWARD GREY, K.G.: By the Author of "King Edward VII."

> The only Life Story ever published of H.M. Secretary of State for Foreign Affairs.

Uniform with the above volumes.

THE REAL CROWN PRINCE: By the Author of "Sir Edward Grey, K.G."

> The Author thoroughly unmasks the early influences which mould and permeate the character of a Prussian monarch.

2/6 net each of all Booksellers, or post free **2/8** direct from

GEORGE NEWNES, Ltd., 8-11 Southampton Street, Strand, W.C.

NEWNES' POPULAR SHILLING SERIES

Artistic Cloth Cover—Coloured Picture Wrapper—Good Paper—Clear Type.

W. W. Jacobs — Salthaven / Master of Craft / Sea Urchins / At Sunwich Port

H. De Vere Stacpoole — The Street of the Flute Player / Drums of War / Ships of Coral

R. W. Chambers — The Common Law / The Danger Mark / Ailsa Paige / The Streets of Ascalon.

Temple Thurston — Apple of Eden / Evolution of Katherine

Humphry Ward — Canadian Born / Diana Mallory

Mrs. Belloc Lowndes — Price of Admiralty / When no Man Pursueth / Studies in Wives

Eden Phillpotts — Forest on the Hill / The Beacon

BEATRICE HARRADEN - Hilda Strafford
JOHN OXENHAM - Maid of the Silver Sea
STANLEY WEYMAN - Count Hannibal
Mrs. E. NESBIT - The House with No Address
FRANK DANBY - Heart of a Child
RENE BAZIN - The Nun
MAY EDGINTON - Oh! James!
J. C. SNAITH - The Principal Girl

1/- net. Of all Booksellers, Newsagents, and Bookstalls, or (postage 2d. extra) from the Publishers—

GEORGE NEWNES, Ltd., 8-11 Southampton Street, Strand, W.C.

The International Reference Atlas of the World

10/6 net

This Splendid Atlas will form a priceless possession to every OFFICER AT THE FRONT

It is thoroughly reliable and singularly complete, and has been produced by His Majesty's Cartographer

J. G. BARTHOLOMEW
LL.D., F.R.G.S., etc.

THE INTERNATIONAL REFERENCE ATLAS OF THE WORLD is entirely new, and contains 120 Modern and Authentic Maps, beautifully printed in colours, with Geographical pronunciation and a general Index of nearly 25,000 Names of Places with latitude and longitude.

10/6 *net of all Booksellers, or* 10/10 *post free from the Publishers*

GEORGE NEWNES, Ltd., 8-11 Southampton Street, Strand, W.C.

DA   Spender, Harold
566   Herbert Henry Asquith
.9
07S72

**PLEASE DO NOT REMOVE
CARDS OR SLIPS FROM THIS POCKET**

ERINDALE COLLEGE LIBRARY